THE COMPLETE TRAEGER GRILL COOKBOOK 2021:

A Mouth-Watering Smoker Cookbook, Master your Traeger skills with 100 Flavorful Step-by-Step Grilled, Crispy Glazed and Roasted Recipes

Steven Franklin

© Copyright 2021 - All rights reserved.

The content contained within this book may not be reproduced, duplicated or transmitted without direct written permission from the author or the publisher.

Under no circumstances will any blame or legal responsibility be held against the publisher, or author, for any damages, reparation, or monetary loss due to the information contained within this book. Either directly or indirectly.

Legal Notice:

This book is copyright protected. This book is only for personal use. You cannot amend, distribute, sell, use, quote or paraphrase any part, or the content within this book, without the consent of the author or publisher.

Disclaimer Notice:

Please note the information contained within this document is for educational and entertainment purposes only. All effort has been executed to present accurate, up to date, and reliable, complete information. No warranties of any kind are declared or implied. Readers acknowledge that the author is not engaging in the rendering of legal, financial, medical or professional advice. The content within this book has been derived from various sources. Please consult a licensed professional before attempting any techniques outlined in this book.

By reading this document, the reader agrees that under no circumstances is the author responsible for any losses, direct or indirect, which are incurred as a result of the use of information contained within this document, including, but not limited to, errors, omissions, or inaccuracies.

Table Of Contents

INTRODUCTION 8
TRAEGER WOOD PELLET GRILL 12
    HOW IT WORKS 13
    TRAEGER WOOD PELLET GRILL VS. CHARCOAL AND WOOD GRILLS 14
    PELLETS TO USE 14
    BENEFITS OF THE WOOD PELLET SMOKER-GRILL 15
WHAT YOU CAN COOK WITH YOUR TRAEGER 18
    COOKING TEMPERATURES, TIMES, AND DONENESS: 20
CLEANING AND MAINTENANCE 22
TIPS TO SUCCEED 24
GRILL BEEF RECIPES 28
    BBQ BRISKET 29
    PRIME RIB ROAST 30
    THAI BEEF SKEWERS 31
    COWBOY CUT STEAK 32
    GRILLED BUTTER BASTED STEAK 33
    CHILI RIB EYE STEAKS 34
    BBQ BEEF SHORT RIBS 35
GRILL PORK RECIPES 36
    SMOKED PORK SHOULDER 36
    ZESTY HERBAL SMOKE PORK TENDERLOIN 37
    PULLED HICKORY-SMOKED PORK BUTTS 38
    PORK SIRLOIN TIP ROAST THREE WAYS 39
    TERIYAKI-MARINATED PORK SIRLOIN TIP ROAST 40
    HICKORY-SMOKED PORK SIRLOIN TIP ROAST 41
    DOUBLE-SMOKED HAM 42
    HICKORY-SMOKED PRIME RIB OF PORK 43
    TENDER GRILLED LOIN CHOPS 44
    FLORENTINE RIBEYE PORK LOIN 45
    NAKED ST. LOUIS RIBS 46
GRILL LAMB RECIPES 48
    TRAEGER SMOKED PULLED LAMB SLIDERS 49
    TRAEGER SMOKED LAMB MEATBALLS 50
    TRAEGER CROWN RACK OF LAMB 51
    TRAEGER SMOKED LEG 52

GRILL POULTRY RECIPES 54

TRADITIONAL THANKSGIVING TURKEY 55
TURKEY JALAPENO MEATBALLS 56
WILD TURKEY SOUTHWEST EGG ROLLS 57
SMOKED WILD TURKEY BREAST 58
GRILLED WILD TURKEY ORANGE CASHEW SALAD 59
BAKED CORNBREAD TURKEY TAMALE PIE 60

TURKEY, RABBIT AND VEAL 62

SMOKE ROASTED CHICKEN 63
GRILLED ASIAN CHICKEN BURGERS 64
GRILLED SWEET CAJUN WINGS 66
THE GRILLED CHICKEN CHALLENGE 67
CHICKEN BREAST WITH LEMON 68
TRAEGER SMOKED CHICKEN BURGERS 69
PERFECT SMOKED CHICKEN PATTIES 70

SMOKING RECIPES 72

SMOKED APPLE PORK BUTT RECIPE 72
SMOKED BEER-CAN TURKEY RECIPE 74
SWEET SMOKED PORK RIBS RECIPE 76
BAKED GREEN BEAN CASSEROLE 77

FISH AND SEAFOOD RECIPES 78

ROASTED YELLOWTAIL 79
BAKED STEELHEAD 80
WINE BRINED SALMON 81
CITRUS SALMON 82
SIMPLE MAHI-MAHI 83
ROSEMARY TROUT 84
SESAME SEEDS FLOUNDER 85
PARSLEY PRAWN SKEWERS 86
BUTTERED SHRIMP 87
PROSCIUTTO WRAPPED SCALLOPS 88
BUTTERED CLAMS 89

VEGETARIAN RECIPES 90

CORN & CHEESE CHILE RELLENOS 91
ROASTED TOMATOES WITH HOT PEPPER SAUCE 92
GRILLED FINGERLING POTATO SALAD 93
SMOKED JALAPEÑO POPPERS 94
GRILLED VEGGIE SANDWICH 95
SMOKED HEALTHY CABBAGE 96

- GARLIC AND ROSEMARY POTATO WEDGES 97
- SMOKED TOMATO AND MOZZARELLA DIP 98
- FEISTY ROASTED CAULIFLOWER 99
- SAVORY APPLESAUCE ON THE GRILL 100

VEGAN RECIPES **102**
- WOOD PELLET SMOKED ACORN SQUASH 103
- WOOD PELLET SMOKED VEGETABLES 104

RED MEAT RECIPES...**106**
- RED WINE BRAISED LAMB 106
- MUSTARD ANCHOVY RIB EYE STEAKS 107

BAKING RECIPES **108**
- BAKED PUMPKIN SEEDS... 109
- CINNAMON PUMPKIN SEEDS 110
- CILANTRO AND LIME CORN 111

CHEESE AND BREAD **112**
- BERRY COBBLER ON A TRAEGER GRILL 112
- TRAEGER GRILL APPLE CRISP 114

APPETIZERS AND SIDES **116**
- MUSHROOMS STUFFED WITH CRAB MEAT... 116
- BACON WRAPPED WITH ASPARAGUS 118
- BACON CHEDDAR SLIDER... 119

MORE SIDES..**120**
- CRANBERRY-ALMOND BROCCOLI SALAD... 120
- ONION BACON RING 121
- GRILLED WATERMELON JUICE 122

SNACKS..**124**
- SMOKED GUACAMOLE 125
- JALAPENO POPPERS.. 126

DESSERT RECIPE...**128**
- PELLET GRILL APPLE CRISP 128
- FROMAGE MACARONI AND CHEESE 129
- SPICY BARBECUE PECANS 130

SAUCES AND RUBS **132**
- CLASSIC HOME-MADE WORCESTERSHIRE SAUCE 132

- Original Ketchup 133
- Lovely Mayonnaise 134

NUT AND FRUIT RECIPES 136
- Grilled Fruit and Cream 136

TRADITIONAL RECIPES 138
- Chicken Casserole 138

SAUCES, RUBS, AND MARINATES 140
- Chimichurri Sauce 140

RUBS, INJECTABLES, MARINADES, AND MOPS 142
- Sweet and Spicy Cinnamon Rub 142
- Wood-Fired Burger Shake 143

OTHER RECIPES YOU NEVER THOUGHT ABOUT TO GRILL 144
- Wild Boar 144
- Honey Apricot Smoked Lamb Shank 145
- Braised Rabbit and Red Wine Stew 146
- Citrus Smoked Goose Breast 147
- Maple-Glazed Pheasants 148
- Ultimate Duck Breasts 149
- Wild Game Chili 150
- Grilled Rabbit with Wine and Rosemary Marinade 151
- Grilled Wild Boar Steaks with Blueberry Sauce 152
- Grilled Wild Goose Breast in Beer Marinade 153
- Grilled Wild Rabbit with Rosemary and Garlic 154
- Stuffed Wild Duck on Pellet Grill 155

CONCLUSION 156

INTRODUCTION

Traeger is a grill and smoker-manufacturing company that is based in Oregon and reputed for using all-natural flavored wood pellets. As far as its origins, Joe Traeger wanted to cook a scrumptious meal for his family when he discovered that his gas grill was burned down.

The very next day, he decided to make a grill with wooden pellets to ensure a fire-free barbeque for the entire summer. As time passed, the first grill by Traeger was mass-produced in 1988.

Subsequently, the company released six different models of barbeque grills, apart from rubs, sauces, spices, smokers, and even apparel. Until 2005, Traeger Grills owned the wood pellet stove patent.

So, how does the Traeger grill work? When you turn the appliance on, the motor starts the rotation of a screw-like device, called the auger, which feeds the burn pot. The pellets then are ignited, and exhaust is via the chimney.

Traeger grills are also fitted with air convection that feeds air to the burning pellets. This ensures that the heat is efficiently distributed and the air around the food is filled with smoke. Similar to a convection oven, the heat is moved around the meat.

Some special aspects of the Traeger Grills are:

1. **The fuel**

Most other types of grills make use of charcoal, natural gas, or propane as a source of fuel. In the case of these fuel sources, the user needs to have a bit of knowledge of the grill type and be present to 'babysit' the grill.

On the other hand, Traeger grills use wood pellets that are all-natural and all-wood. These pellets can burn well in a controlled environment and provide flavorful food. Additionally, these pellets are FDA-approved and safe for home and outdoor uses.

The pellets are available in 14 distinct flavors. They can be used to create a new range of individual flavors and do not harm the environment when burned.

2. Flavor

Traeger pellets are available in 14 different types of pellets like pecan, apple, mesquite, hickory, etc. Apart from infusing delicious flavor to the meat, you can also use them for baking sweets like pie and cookies.

3. No flare-up

There are no flare-ups in roasting, baking, smoking, or grilling when you are using indirect electric heat, not gas. This is because electric heat (indirect) does not lead to flare-ups. The appliances are also not exposed to dripping temperatures.

4. Control of the temperature

One of the best aspects of the Traeger Grill is total control of the temperature. Once you set it, the grill is capable of maintaining consistent heat, even if the weather may not look favorable.

The Traeger grills can be set in 5-degree increments, which is a feature not seen in many grills, especially charcoal and gas ones. All you need to do is cook the food using the recipe and not worry about the appliance dropping down the temperature.

Additionally, since pellets are essentially electric, you are not tied to your grill like a gas grill. For instance, you do not have to keep checking the grill from time-to-time to ensure that the food has not burned.

5. Environmentally-friendly

Grills manufactured by Traeger make use of all-natural and real wood pellets that can burn within a controlled system, thereby offering flavor, ease of use, and convenience.

These grills are also approved by the FDA and the flavors of the pellets can be blended to create a mix of flavors. Additionally, burning these pellets will not cause any harm to the environment, as mentioned before.

The picture of a good time with loved ones, neighbors and friends having a backyard barbeque is a pretty sight, isn't it? Having a smoker-grill and some grilled and smoked recipes are excellent when you have visitors at home, because you can deliver both tasty food and magical moment on a summer night, for example. Hundreds of awesome recipes are available that you can try with a wood pellet smoker-grill! Experiment, improve, or make your own recipes – it is up to you. You can do it fast and easy. But if you want to be safe with the proven and tested ones, by all means do so. These recipes have been known to be just right to the taste and they work every time. A combination of creating a correct impression the first time and every time and enjoying scrumptious food along the way will be your edge.

TRAEGER WOOD PELLET GRILL

Traeger Wood Pellet Grill is a wood pellet grill that has a set of manual controls that allows the user to control the cooking temperature. It differs from other smoker grills such as the Traeger electric smoker and the pellet grills that use a digital control to adjust the temperature. The grill uses a wood pellet fuel that causes it to smoke. The different types of wood pellets that the grill uses to smoke food are Apple wood pellets, Hickory wood pellets, Mesquite wood pellets, Cherry wood pellets, and Alder wood pellets. The wood pellets can be used to smoke chicken, turkey, fish, oysters, cow beef, and many other types of poultry. The wood pellets can be used to smoke other foods such as pizza, vegetables, and other foods. The wood pellets are made using recycled wood materials. The wood pellet grill can also be used to grill foods and bake foods. The grill is easy to use because it's made of a simple design and it doesn't have any complicated elements. The Traeger wood pellet grill is easy to use and can be used indoors as well as outdoors. The user can check the temperature to make sure that the food is cooked perfectly. Most types of the grill can be used both as gas grills and charcoal grills.

One of the popular features of the Traeger wood pellet grill is the result of its smoke from the wood pellet. Many customers are amazed by the wood pellet smoker. There are hundreds of positive and amazing testimonials about the grill. The grill allows users to smoke and grill their food and the meat can be smoked for up to 15 hours. The grill is easy to use, functional, and reliable. The Traeger grill is also very durable because of its body. The body of the grill is made of cast iron. The BBQ grill is easy to install and is easy to maintain. The grill can create smoke by using wood pellets and it can be adjusted to a temperature of about 225 degrees Fahrenheit. The food cooked on the grill has a consistent smoky flavor because of the wood pellets. The grill is an automatic cooker, meaning it conserves the heat that it produces, and it doesn't lose heat.

How It Works

Many people try to grill using real firewood methods while grilling in the Traeger grill. But they do not know how to use Traeger grill with wood pellets. Let's first see how Traeger pellet grill works.

To start with Traeger grill, user has to open the lid and set the temperature at 250 and make the grill smoke by turning it on. It has to be set as 250 for first 30 mins. User also has to turn on the heat of the grill and grill meat or food, which you want to use. The smoke has to be essential for cooking with pellets. If Traeger grill is not important to work with, then user can also set the smoker for working with the Traeger pellets.

It will not work without smoke. So, first thing to do is get the griller hot and the smoker working. The temperature will rise up to 260. The grill grates are placed on the grill so as to let the smoke pass through the meat while cooking. The temperature will rise up to 260, if one is not able to control it, be sure to turn off the barbecue grill. The Traeger grill is very simple to use and it is quite easy to control the temperature.

Once you want to know how to use Traeger grill and smoke, you will be able to find it quite easy and all you need to do is to open the lid and then set the temperature. Switch on the smoke for the first time so that smoke can come out and cook the food.

It is the same as the way how to use Traeger pellet grill for smoking

So, if you want to do BBQs for your family, then Traeger grill is the best choice to use. It has a capacity to hold about seventeen burgers. So, one can easily do a party or BBQ night for quite large crowd. The food will be very tasty, once it is ready with Traeger pellet grill.

Traeger Wood Pellet Grill Vs. Charcoal and Wood Grills

Traeger wood pallets have numerous benefits that other charcoal and gas grill cannot provide. Barbecuing is a great gathering excuse and outdoor activity, but it is a hassle to set. In this day and age where everything is becoming more convenient, this activity should also become easier to deal with as well.

It is easy to start:

To get a charcoal or gas grill to ignite is a hassle, but the fire inside firepot is easy to turn on. It also is much safer as you don't have to stick your hands inside the grill to start the fire.

It's versatile

This grill is not only used for grilling but can be used for different processes of cooking as well. You can bake, roast, smoke, and braise using this device. This also increases the menu at your barbecue gathering.

No burnt areas

Because the cooking process happens by convection mechanism, the entire piece of meat, or whatever your cooking gets cooked evenly. There is also no need to flip around the meat constantly. Also, the drip tray prevents direct fire from hitting your food, so no charring occurs.

More flavor in your dishes

In grilling, nothing beats all-natural hardwood flavor. Professional chefs use them, and now, with ease, so could you. It is not hard to produce a much more delicious juicy meat steak at your home anymore.

Pellets to Use

The dark charcoal type of wood pellets is used to cook food. They are burned to cook food inside it. It is made of a variety of woods like beech, maple, and cherry that has a composition of 15 - 20 percent mesquite, it burns at 1400 degrees. The process to burn wood pellets is very simple. You need to pour it to a box, add in the grill and light it with matchstick, then it will burn to give you the best flavor. The burning wood pellets will provide you the warmth and keep you surrounded with the great and the best natural flavor. This is the burning pellets or the logs that make the grills unique.

Benefits of the Wood Pellet Smoker-Grill

There are several advantages to using a wood pellet smoker-grill. Not only does it enhance the taste of your food, but it also offers several other benefits. Here are some of the biggest benefits of a wood pellet smoker-grill!

Saves Time

It is a no-brainer that anything that saves time as well as effort, especially when it comes to cooking, deserves a warm welcome. One of the biggest advantages of using wood pellet grills is that they save you a lot of time. You can make your smoked dishes much faster and with much more ease and comfort. You can pre-heat them quickly, so you will save a lot of time.

Offers Varied Cooking Options

The best thing about wood pellet smoker-grills is that they give you several options for easy cooking. They are versatile and let you easily experiment with recipes and food. You can try various smoked recipes on the grill and enjoy healthy cooking. The versatility of pellet grills is probably one of their best qualities. This ensures that you can enjoy several lip-smacking recipes in a matter of minutes. In addition, you can use pellet grills to cook all kinds of food, from braised short ribs to chicken wings.

Offers Variety

Another significant advantage of using a wood pellet smoker-grill is that these smokers and grills come in a plethora of sizes and shapes. These grills are built and designed keeping the preferences, needs, and tastes of customers in mind. Therefore, people who are looking for convenient cooking tools can always find something for themselves in wood pellet smokers and grills. You can also choose from a wide range of flavors, such as maple, pecan, hickory, apple, and much more.

Cold Smoking

In addition to wood pellet fire grills and smokers, you can buy cold smokers from some companies. You can cook salmon and cheese dishes in these cold smokers.

Ease of Use

It is common to see many people get intimidated by the idea of using a pellet grill. However, those fears are unfounded. While a pellet grill is quite different from your standard charcoal grills or gas grills, they are surprisingly easy to use.

These grills come with controls that users can set and then simply forget about. They come with several features that make the entire process of grilling a piece of cake.

These grills usually do not require any lighter fluid and they start with a single button. In addition, irrespective of the weather or the temperature outside, these grills can keep the temperature within a 10-degree range of your set temperature. This allows you to cook with zero effort like a pro. These grills are also designed to ensure that you do not overcook or over-smoke your food. Plus, they never flare up. So, there is no need for you to worry about your beautiful eyebrows.

Value

While pellet smokers are slightly more expensive than standard grills, this is for a good reason. As mentioned above, these pieces of equipment offer the perfect combination of a smoker and a grill. They come with solid construction and stainless-steel components. This is precisely why they also come with a nice four-year warranty.

This means that you will not buy these grills for a summer only to dispose of them come winter. In addition, fuel efficiency is another one of their advantages. They come packed with double-wall insulation, which helps them sustain their temperatures better as well as use less fuel.

So, what are you waiting for? If you like to smoke or grill your food, it is not possible to go wrong with a good-quality pellet grill. They provide a wide range of advantages, such as their ease of use and the incredible flavor of your favorite smoked wood. Therefore, these grills are an amazing value for the money.

Keeping this in mind, let us dive right into some amazing tried-and-tested recipes using a wood pellet smoker-grill!

WHAT YOU CAN COOK WITH YOUR TRAEGER

What makes a wood pellet smoker and grill unique is the very thing that fuels it -- wood pellets. Wood pellets are compressed sawdust, made from pine wood, birch wood, fir wood, or crop stalks. Culinary-wise, wood pellets are used mostly as fuel for pellet smokers and grills, although they can also be used for household heating. What makes wood pellets for cooking special, though, is that they come in flavors. And speaking of flavors, here is a quick wood pellet flavor guide for you:

Apple & Cherry Pellets: These pellets possess a smoky, mild, sweet flavor. They can enhance mild meat and are usually the go-to flavor for cooking pork or poultry. Despite being able to produce great Smoke, these pellets are very mild.

Alder Pellets: This type of pellet is mild and neutral, but with some sweetness in it. If you're looking for something that provides a good amount of Smoke but won't overpower delicate meat like chicken and fish, this is the flavor to go to.

Hickory Pellets: Hickory pellets produce a rich, Smokey, and bacon-like flavor. These are the pellets that are widely used for barbecue. Since this type of pellet is rich and Smokey, it can tend to be overwhelming. If that is the case, consider mixing it with apple or oak pellets.

Maple Pellets: If you are looking for something that is mild and comes with a hint of sweetness, maple pellets are the best option for you. They are great to use on turkey or pork.

Mesquite Pellets: A favorite option for Texas BBQ, mesquite pellets, is characterized by a strong, spicy, and tangy flavor.

Oak Pellets: Oak pellets come in between apple and Hickory. They are a bit stronger than the former and a bit milder than the latter and are an excellent choice when you're cooking fish or vegetables.

Pecan Pellets: Pecan is an all-time favorite. It's very similar to Hickory, but with a touch of Vanilla, nutty flavor. The perfect pellets for beef and chicken, pecan pellets are very palatable and suits all of

Qualities of a Good Brand of Wood Pellets

With the hundreds of different wood pellets' varieties and brands, it is often difficult to identify which brand to consider. If you are not sure what brand to opt for, it might help try at least the top three brands you know of and compare their efficiency. Appearance: The first factor to consider when choosing a brand of wood pellets is the appearance of the pellets. After using wood pellets for some time, you will be able to tell and judge their quality simply by how they appear. The first thing to check is the length of the pellets. Brands adhere to certain standards, so this is not a concern. Nevertheless, you need to understand that when it comes to pellet fuels, length matters, affecting the performance of the pellets. The dust you will find in the packaging is also another to consider. It is normal to see fines once you open the bag, but if there are an unusual number of fines, it means the pellets aren't of good quality.

Texture: The texture of the pellets is another thing. Wood pellets have a particular texture in them. If you feel that the pellets are smooth and shiny, it means they are of good quality. The same is true if the pellets do not have cracks. If the pellets are too rough with unusual racks on the surface, it means the pellets are bad. This is usually a result of incorrect pressing ratio and moisture content of the raw materials used in making the pellets. Smell: Wood pellets are made by exposing them to high temperatures within a sealed space. During the process, the lignin contained in the biomass material is mixed with other elements, producing a smell of burnt fresh wood. If the pellets smell bad, there is a big chance they have not been appropriately processed or contain impure, raw material. Aside from the appearance, texture, and smell of the wood pellets, another way to check their quality is to see how they react with water. Place a handful of pellets in a bowl of water and allow them to settle for several minutes. If the pellets dissolve in the water and expand quickly, this means they are of good quality. On the other hand, if the pellets do not dissolve within minutes but instead expand and become hard, it means they are of bad quality. Finally, try burning some of the pellets, as well. If the wood pellets are of excellent quality, the flame they produce will be bright and brown. If the flame they make, on the other hand, is dark in color, it means the quality of the pellets is not good. Also, good-quality pellets produce a little ash, so if the pellets leave you with many residues, it is a sign that the pellets are bad.

Cooking Temperatures, Times, and Doneness:

With so many recipes to try with your pellet grill, it is easy to get overwhelmed right away. One important thing to keep in mind is that lower temperatures produce Smoke, while higher temperatures do not. Follow this useful guide below to know the temperature and time required to get the perfectly flavored meat each time.

- Beef briskets are best cooked at 250 degrees using the smoke setting for at least 4 hours by itself and covered with foil for another 4 hours.

- Pork ribs should be cooked at 275 degrees on the smoke setting for 3 hours and covered with foil for another 2-3 hours.

- Steaks require 400-450 degrees for about 10 minutes on each side.

- Turkey can be cooked at 375 degrees for 20 minutes per pound of meat. For smoked turkey, the heat settings should be around 180-225 degrees for 10-12 hours or until the turkeys inside reaches 165 degrees.

- Chicken breasts can be cooked at 400-450 degrees for 15 minutes on each side.

- A whole chicken cooks at 400-450 degrees for 1.5 hours or until the internal temperature reaches 165 degrees.

- Bacon and Sausage can be cooked at 425 degrees for 5-8 minutes on each side.

- Hamburgers should be cooked at 350 degrees for at least 8 minutes for each side.

- You can smoke salmon for 1-1.5 hours and finish with a high setting for 2-3 minutes on each side.

- Shrimps cook at 400-450 degrees for 3-5 minutes on each side. If you prefer a smokier flavor, set the temperature at 225 degrees for about 30 minutes.

Wood to Meat Pairing Chart

FLAVOR	BEEF	PORK	SEAFOOD	LAMB	GAME MEAT
Apple		X	X	X	
Alder		X		X	
Hickory	X	X		X	X
Mesquite	X	X	X		
Oak		X		X	X
Pecan	X	X		X	X

CLEANING AND MAINTENANCE

All equipment, including a grill smoker, needs to be taken care of. Especially if you're serious about smoking and want your equipment to last.

The main difference between smokers and grills is the temperature at which the food is cooked. A smoker cooks food at a low temperature (about 225 degrees F) and a grill cooks it at 300 degrees F or higher. The reason this is important is that when food is cooked at a lower temperature, the metal needs to be taken better care of that the metal of grills that use high heat. With a grill, the high heat can incinerate most cooking grease left behind in the fire chamber while the lower heat of the smoker is unable to do that, so the grease remains.

3 rules when using a smoker:

A brand-new smoker needs to be seasoned before use

To season a smoker, you first need to coat the inside surface with some kind of cooking oil or bacon grease.

When that oil is heated, it will seep into all the pores of the metal surface of the smoker. This will create a barrier that prevents rusting.

You need to heat the smoker to a temperature of about 250-275 degrees F. Don't goes above this temperature as you may damage the paint. You can use charcoal but it's better to use the sort of fuel you plan to use for smoking food. Keep the smoker at this temperature for 2-3 hours.

Seasoning is essential because it destroys all the chemicals used during the manufacturing process so even if the instruction book does not insist on seasoning, it's better to fire up your smoker than not. That way you'll be sure your food is free of toxins.

A smoker will occasionally have to be repaired and repainted

From time to time, even if you are not using it very often, your smoker will need to be cleaned. Remove all the rust by scrubbing it with a wire brush and sandpaper. Clean it thoroughly and repaint it with heat resistant barbecue paint. A good-quality smoker can last many decades, i.e. a lifetime, provided you take good care of it. Don't forget that the state of your smoker affects the taste of the food you prepare in it. Therefore, routine maintenance is essential.

It needs to be cleaned after each and every use

Taking care of your smoker means you will have to keep it clean by removing the ash and not allow food build-up. However, although a smoker requires occasional scrubbing, the protective coating must not be damaged so you should never scrub the smoker down to the bare metal.

If you've had it for a long time or use it often, you may need to thoroughly clean it out and season it from time to time. To prevent rusting, you need to maintain the smoky, oily surface over the metal.

Ash should never be allowed to remain in the smoker after it's been used, as it can absorb water and lead to rusting. Large deposits of grease trapped against the metal need to be scraped gently. A clean and looked-after smoker not only has a longer life but it also makes your food taste better.

TIPS TO SUCCEED

Tips and Tricks for Using Your Traeger Grill

If you are looking for some tips and tricks that can help you better utilize your Traeger grill, they are listed for you. If you already have the appliance, you are already on the sweet side of life. Whether you are a grill newbie or a master, there are always things that you can learn to become the ultimate grill and smoker master.

Some of the top tricks, tips, and hacks that can make your barbequing, smoking, and grilling experience better include:

1. Always use disposable drip bucket liners

If you get tired of cleaning up that slimy residue every time you decide to grill or smoke some steak or are prone to bumping the bucket off accidentally when putting on the cover, it is recommended that you look for bucket liners - disposable ones of course. With the help of these disposable drip bucket liners, cleaning will become much easier.

2. Grill lights to light the way

If you plan on cooking at night or are always bumping around the grill in the dark, you can look for some grill lights. If you are a serious smoker but are busy dealing with the headlamp or flashlight, these grill lights will come in very handy.

No wonder this device is one of the top-sellers on several online shopping sites. The grill lights are fitted with a magnetic base and can clamp and bend according to the shape of the grill.

3. Drip tray liners for easier cleaning

If you want to get serious, then it is time to dump the aluminum foil. Once you have the drip tray liners, you will not have to deal with wadded up, oily, blackened, or small tears in the foil.

The overall idea here is to make the cleaning process easier so that you can redirect your focus on the more important things, such as smoking and grilling.

4. Meat temperature and meat smoking magnets to measure the temperature accurately

One of the worst things that can happen while grilling and smoking meat is guessing the cooking temperature. With the help of meat smoking and temperature magnets, you can now leave all the frantic web searches behind.

With these devices, you will know the internal temperature that you need to cook meat safely. Then, you will always have perfectly cooked pieces of meat all the time.

5. Wireless thermometer or Tappecue for the perfect temperature

You have already spent hundreds of dollars on a perfect grill. However, you can still end up spending tens and thousands of dollars more each time you decide to cook on it.

If you want to protect your important investment from harm, you need to ensure that you do not have to 'peek' while cooking. With the Tappecue, you will get the internal temperature that you are looking for.

6. Swap out pellets with bucket head vacuum

Imagine that you need to move from the apple to the hickory flavor. However, you see that the grill is more than half-full of apple pellets. What can do you in this scenario? Of course, you can choose to wait until the pellets cool down and then remove them. Another solution to this issue is using a bucket head vacuum.

Once done, you will be left with storage that you can use any time. Additionally, you do not even need a specialized bucket for this purpose; you can use a simple bucket and storage lid kit that is fitted with a filter.

7. Add extra smoke on any type of cooking with an A-maze-n Smoker Tube

If you love smoking, you should definitely buy a dedicated smoker tube – like the A-maze-n Smoker Tube. Known for its great simplicity, this tube is one of the best tools for a seasoned smoker. All you need to do is to add some pellets and light it at just one end. Then, leave it on the grates.

A smoker tube is a great option for cold smoking fish, nuts, and cheese; of course, it can also be used for some extra smoke on meats, like brisket, pulled pork, etc.

GRILL BEEF RECIPES

BBQ Brisket

Preparation Time: 12 hours

Cooking Time: 10 hours

Servings: 8

Ingredients:

- 1 beef brisket, about 12 pounds
- Beef rub as needed

Directions:

1. Season beef brisket with beef rub until well coated, place it in a large plastic bag, seal it and let it marinate for a minimum of 12 hours in the refrigerator.
2. When ready to cook, switch on the Traeger grill, fill the grill hopper with hickory flavored traegers, power the grill on by using the control panel, select 'smoke' on the temperature dial, or set the temperature to 225 degrees F and let it preheat for a minimum of 15 minutes.
3. When the grill has preheated, open the lid, place marinated brisket on the grill grate fat-side down, shut the grill, and smoke for 6 hours until the internal temperature reaches 160 degrees F.
4. Then wrap the brisket in foil, return it back to the grill grate and cook for 4 hours until the internal temperature reaches 204 degrees F.
5. When done, transfer brisket to a cutting board, let it rest for 30 minutes, then cut it into slices and serve.

Nutrition: Calories: 328 Cal Fat: 21 g Protein: 32 g

Prime Rib Roast

Preparation Time: 24 hours

Cooking Time: 4 hours and 30 minutes

Servings: 8

Ingredients:

- 1 prime rib roast, containing 5 to 7 bones
- Rib rub as needed

Directions:

1. Season rib roast with rib rub until well coated, place it in a large plastic bag, seal it and let it marinate for a minimum of 24 hours in the refrigerator.
2. When ready to cook, switch on the Traeger grill, fill the grill hopper with cherry flavored traegers, power the grill on by using the control panel, select 'smoke' on the temperature dial, or set the temperature to 225 degrees F and let it preheat for a minimum of 15 minutes.
3. When the grill has preheated, open the lid, place rib roast on the grill grate fat-side up, change the smoking temperature to 425 degrees F, shut the grill, and smoke for 30 minutes.
4. Then change the smoking temperature to 325 degrees F and continue cooking for 3 to 4 hours until roast has cooked to the desired level, rare at 120 degrees F, medium rare at 130 degrees F, medium at 140 degrees F, and well done at 150 degrees F.
5. When done, transfer roast rib to a cutting board, let it rest for 15 minutes, then cut it into slices and serve.

Nutrition: Calories: 248 Cal Fat: 21.2 g Protein: 28 g

Thai Beef Skewers

Preparation Time: 15 minutes

Cooking Time: 8 minutes

Servings: 6

Ingredients:

- ½ of medium red bell pepper, destemmed, cored, cut into a ¼-inch piece
- ½ of beef sirloin, fat trimmed
- ½ cup salted peanuts, roasted, chopped
- 1 teaspoon minced garlic
- 1 tablespoon grated ginger
- 1 lime, juiced
- 1 teaspoon ground black pepper
- 1 tablespoon sugar
- 1/4 cup soy sauce
- 1/4 cup olive oil

Directions:

1. Prepare the marinade and for this, take a small bowl, place all of its ingredients in it, whisk until combined, and then pour it into a large plastic bag.
2. Cut into beef sirloin 1-1/4-inch dice, add to the plastic bag containing marinade, seal the bag, turn it upside down to coat beef pieces with the marinade and let it marinate for a minimum of 2 hours in the refrigerator.
3. When ready to cook, switch on the Traeger grill, fill the grill hopper with cherry flavored traegers, power the grill on by using the control panel, select 'smoke' on the temperature dial, or set the temperature to 425 degrees F and let it preheat for a minimum of 5 minutes.
4. Meanwhile, remove beef pieces from the marinade and then thread onto skewers.
5. When the grill has preheated, open the lid, place prepared skewers on the grill grate, shut the grill, and smoke for 4 minutes per side until done.
6. When done, transfer skewers to a dish, sprinkle with peanuts and red pepper, and then serve.

Nutrition: Calories: 124 Cal Fat: 5.5 g Carbs: 1.7 g Protein: 15.6 g Fiber: 0 g

Cowboy Cut Steak

Preparation Time: 10 minutes

Cooking Time: 1 hour and 15 minutes

Servings: 4

Ingredients:

- 2 cowboy cut steak, each about 2 ½ pounds
- Salt as needed
- Beef rub as needed
- For the Gremolata:
- 2 tablespoons chopped mint
- 1 bunch of parsley, leaves separated
- 1 lemon, juiced
- 1 tablespoon lemon zest
- ½ teaspoon minced garlic
- ¼ teaspoon salt
- 1/8 teaspoon ground black pepper
- 1/4 cup olive oil

Directions:

1. Switch on the Traeger grill, fill the grill hopper with mesquite flavored traegers, power the grill on by using the control panel, select 'smoke' on the temperature dial, or set the temperature to 225 degrees F and let it preheat for a minimum of 5 minutes.
2. When done, transfer steaks to a dish, let rest for 15 minutes, and meanwhile, change the smoking temperature of the grill to 450 degrees F and let it preheat for a minimum of 10 minutes.
3. Then return steaks to the grill grate and cook for 7 minutes per side until the internal temperature reaches 130 degrees F.

Nutrition: Calories: 361 Cal Fat: 31 g Carbs: 1 g Protein: 19 g Fiber: 0.2 g

Grilled Butter Basted Steak

Preparation Time: 10 minutes

Cooking Time: 40 minutes

Servings: 2

Ingredients:

- 2 steaks, each about 16 ounces, 1 ½-inch thick
- Rib rub as needed
- 2 teaspoon Dijon mustard
- 2 tablespoons Worcestershire sauce
- 4 tablespoons butter, unsalted, melted

Directions:

1. Switch on the Traeger grill, fill the grill hopper with hickory traegers, power the grill on by using the control panel, select 'smoke' on the temperature dial, or set the temperature to 225 degrees F and let it preheat for a minimum of 15 minutes.
2. Then return steaks to the grill grate and cook for 3 minutes per side until the internal temperature reaches 140 degrees F.
3. Transfer steaks to a dish, let rest for 5 minutes and then serve.

Nutrition: Calories: 409.8 Cal Fat: 30.8 g Carbs: 3.1 g Protein: 29.7 g Fiber: 0.4 g

Chili Rib Eye Steaks

Preparation Time: 10 minutes

Cooking Time: 1 hour

Servings: 4

Ingredients:

- 4 rib-eye steaks, each about 12 ounces
- 1 tablespoon minced garlic
- 1 teaspoon salt
- 1 teaspoon brown sugar
- 2 tablespoons red chili powder
- 1 teaspoon ground cumin
- 2 tablespoons Worcestershire sauce
- 2 tablespoons olive oil

Directions:

1. Prepare the rub and for this, take a small bowl, place all of its ingredients in it and then stir until mixed.
2. Brush the paste on all sides of the steak, rub well, then place steaks into a plastic bag and let it marinate for a minimum of 4 hours.
3. Then return steaks to the grill grate and cook for 3 minutes per side until the internal temperature reaches 140 degrees F.
4. Transfer steaks to a dish, let rest for 5 minutes and then serve.

Nutrition: Calories: 293 Cal Fat: 0 g Protein: 32 g

BBQ Beef Short Ribs

Preparation Time: 15 minutes

Cooking Time: 10 hours

Servings: 8

Ingredients:

- 4 beef short rib racks, membrane removed, containing 4 bones
- 1/2 cup beef rub
- 1 cup apple juice

Directions:

1. Switch on the Traeger grill, fill the grill hopper with apple-flavored traegers, power the grill on by using the control panel, select 'smoke' on the temperature dial, or set the temperature to 225 degrees F and let it preheat for a minimum of 15 minutes.
2. Meanwhile, prepare the ribs, and for this, sprinkle beef rub on both sides until well coated.
3. When the grill has preheated, open the lid, place ribs on the grill grate bone-side down, shut the grill, and smoke for 10 hours until internal temperature reaches 205 degrees F, spritzing with apple juice every hour.
4. When done, transfer ribs to a cutting board, let rest for 10 minutes, then cut into slices and serve.

Nutrition: Calories: 280 Cal Fat: 15 g Carbs: 17 g Protein: 20 g Fiber: 1 g

GRILL PORK RECIPES

Smoked Pork Shoulder

Preparation Time: 30 minutes

Cooking Time: 1 hour 30 minutes

Servings: 6

Ingredients:

- 3 pounds pork shoulder, roasts
- Shoulder Rub Ingredients
- 1/4 cup brown sugar
- ¼ cup white sugar
- 1 tablespoon paprika
- 1 tablespoon garlic powder
- Salt, to taste
- ½ tablespoon chili powder
- 1 teaspoon cayenne pepper
- ¼ teaspoon black pepper
- 2 teaspoons dried oregano
- 2 teaspoons cumin
- Liquid Ingredients to Be Injected
- 3/4 cup apple juice
- 1 cup of water
- 1/2 cup sugar
- Salt, to taste
- 6 tablespoons Worcestershire sauce

Directions:

1. Take a large bowl and add all the shoulder spice rub ingredients and mix well.
2. Take a separate bowl and add all the liquid ingredients.
3. Now use an injector to inject the mixed liquid into the meat.
4. Pat dry it from the top with a paper towel.
5. Rub the spice mixture on top and left for a few hours before cooking.
6. Preheat the smoker grill for 50 minutes at 220 degrees F.
7. Put the meat onto the grill grate and cook for 2 hours at 225 degrees.
8. Serve and enjoy.

Nutrition: Calories: 236 kCal Protein: 17 g Fat: 18 g

Zesty Herbal Smoke Pork Tenderloin

Preparation Time: 30 minutes

Cooking Time: 3 hours

Servings: 4

Ingredients:

- 2-4 pork tenderloins
- 6 tablespoons of BBQ sauce
- Pork Rub Ingredients
- The ½ cup of cane sugar
- 1/3 teaspoon of chili powder
- ¼ tablespoon of granulated onion
- ½ tablespoon of granulated garlic
- 1 tablespoon of dried chilies
- 1 tablespoon of dill weed
- 1 tablespoon of lemon powder
- 1 tablespoon mustard powder

Directions:

1. Take a large mixing bowl and combine all the poke rub ingredients in it.
2. Now preheat the smoker grill at 225 degrees Fahrenheit until the smoke started to form
3. Cooking Time for 3 hours, until the internal temperature reaches 150 degrees Fahrenheit.
4. After 3 hours a brush generous amount of the barbecue sauce and then left it to sit for 20 minutes before serving.
5. Serve and enjoy.

Nutrition: Calories: 147 kCal Protein: 26 g Fat: 4 g

Pulled Hickory-Smoked Pork Butts

Preparation Time: 30 to 45 minutes

Cooking Time: 6 hours

Servings: 20

Ingredients:

Traeger: Hickory

- 2 (10-pound) boneless pork butts, vacuum-stuffed or fresh
- 1 cup roasted garlic–seasoned extra-virgin olive oil
- ¾ cup Pork Dry Rub, Jan's Original Dry Rub, or your preferred pork rub

Directions:

1. Trim the fat cap and any effectively available enormous segments of abundance fat from every pork butt as you see fit.
2. Remove the pork butts from the grill and double wrap everyone in heavy-duty aluminum foil. Take care to ensure that you keep your meat probes in the butts as you double-wrap them.
3. Return the wrapped pork butts to your 350°F traeger smoker-grill.
4. Keep cooking the foil-wrapped pork butts until the internal temperature of the pork butts arrives at 200°F to 205°F.
5. Remove the pork butts and FTC them for 3 to 4 hours before pulling and serving.
6. Force the smoked pork butts into minimal succulent shreds utilizing your preferred pulling technique. I prefer utilizing my hands while wearing heat-safe gloves.
7. On the off chance that you'd like, blend the pulled pork butts with any remaining fluids.
8. Serve the pulled pork with grill sauce on a fresh-prepared move topped with coleslaw, or serve the pulled pork with fixings like lettuce, tomato, red onion, mayo, cheese, and horseradish.

Nutrition: Calories: 267 kCal Protein: 25 g Fat: 18 g

Pork Sirloin Tip Roast Three Ways

Preparation Time: 20 minutes

Cooking Time: 1½ to 3 hours

Servings: 4 to 6

Ingredients:

Traeger: Apple, Hickory

- Apple-injected Roasted Pork Sirloin Tip Roast
- 1 (1½ to 2 pounds) pork sirloin tip roast
- ¾ cup 100% apple juice
- 2 tablespoons roasted garlic–seasoned extra-virgin olive oil
- 5 tablespoons Pork Dry Rub or a business rub, for example, Plowboys BBQ Bovine Bold

Directions:

1. Dry the roast with a piece of paper
2. Utilize a flavor/marinade injector to infuse all zones of tip roast with the apple juice.
3. Rub the whole roast with the olive oil and afterward cover generously with the rub.
4. Utilize 2 silicone nourishment grade cooking groups or butcher's twine to support the roast.
5. Roast the meat until the internal temperature arrives at 145°F, about 1½ hours.
6. Rest the roast under a free foil tent for 15 minutes.
7. Remove the cooking groups or twine and cut the roast contrary to what would be expected.

Nutrition: Calories: 354 kCal Protein: 22 g Fat: 30 g

Teriyaki-Marinated Pork Sirloin Tip Roast

Preparation Time: 45 minutes

Cooking Time: 2 hours 30 minutes

Servings: 4

Ingredients:

- 1 (1½ to 2 pounds) pork sirloin tip roast
- Teriyaki marinade, for example, Mr. Yoshida's Original Gourmet Marinade

Directions:

1. Dry the roast with a piece of paper
2. Utilizing a 1-gallon cooler stockpiling sack or a sealable compartment, spread the roast with the teriyaki marinade.
3. Refrigerate medium-term, turning at regular intervals whenever the situation allows.
4. Smoke the meat for 1 hour at 180°F.
5. After 60 minutes, increase your pit temperature to 325°F.
6. Cook the roast until the internal temperature, at the thickest part of the roast, arrives at 145°F, around 1 to 1½ hours.
7. Rest the roast under a free foil tent for 15 minutes.
8. Remove the cooking groups or twine and cut the roast contrary to what would be expected.

Nutrition: Calories: 214 kCal Protein: 17 g Fat: 19 g

Hickory-Smoked Pork Sirloin Tip Roast

Preparation Time: 30 minutes

Cooking Time: 3 hours

Servings: 3

Ingredients:

- 1 (1½ to 2 pounds) pork sirloin tip roast
- 2 tablespoons roasted garlic–seasoned extra-virgin olive oil
- 5 tablespoons Jan's Original Dry Rub, Pork Dry Rub, or your preferred pork rub

Directions:

1. Pat the roast dry with a paper towel.
2. Rub the whole roast with the olive oil. Coat the roast with the rub.
3. Support the roast utilizing 2 to 3 silicone nourishment grade cooking groups or butcher's twine to ensure the roast keeps up its shape during cooking.
4. Wrap the tip roast in plastic wrap and refrigerate medium-term.
5. Place the roast directly on the grill grates and smoke the roast until the internal temperature, at the thickest part of the roast, arrives at 145°F, around 3 hours.
6. Rest the roast under a free foil tent for 15 minutes.
7. Remove the cooking groups or twine and cut the roast contrary to what would be expected.

Nutrition: Calories: 276 kCal Protein: 28 g Fat: 12 g

Double-Smoked Ham

Preparation Time: 15 minutes

Cooking Time: 2½ to 3 hours

Servings: 8 to 12

Ingredients:

- Traeger: Apple, Hickory
- 1 (10-pound) applewood-smoked, boneless, wholly cooked, ready-to-eat ham or bone-in smoked ham

Directions:

1. Remove the ham from its bundling and let sit at room temperature for 30 minutes.
2. Arrange the traeger smoker-grill for a non-direct cooking and preheat to 180°F utilizing apple or hickory traegers relying upon what sort of wood was utilized for the underlying smoking.
3. Place the ham directly on the grill grates and smoke the ham for 1 hour at 180°F.
4. After 60 minutes, increase pit temperature to 350°F.
5. Cooking Time the ham until the internal temperature arrives at 140°F, about 1½ to 2 additional hours.
6. Remove the ham and wrap in foil for 15 minutes before cutting contrary to what would be expected.

Nutrition: Calories: 215 kCal Protein: 21 g Fat: 19 g

Hickory-Smoked Prime Rib of Pork

Preparation Time: 30 minutes

Cooking Time: 3 hours

Servings: 6

Ingredients:

Traeger: Hickory

- 1 (5-pound) rack of pork, around 6 ribs
- ¼ cup roasted garlic–enhanced extra-virgin olive oil
- 6 tablespoons Jan's Original Dry Rub, Pork Dry Rub, or your preferred pork roast rub

Directions:

1. Trim of the fat cap and silver skin from the rack of pork. Much the same as a chunk of ribs a rack of pork has a membrane on the bones. Remove the membrane from the bones by working a spoon handle under the bone membrane until you can get the membrane with a paper towel to pull it off.
2. Rub the olive oil generously on all sides of the meat. Season with the rub, covering all sides of the meat.
3. Double wrap the seasoned rack of pork in plastic wrap and refrigerate for 2 to 4 hours or medium-term.
4. Remove the seasoned rack of pork from the refrigerator and let sit at room temperature for 30 minutes before cooking.
5. Arrange the traeger smoker-grill for a non-direct cooking and preheat to 225°F utilizing hickory traegers.
6. Add your traeger smoker-grill meat probe or a remote meat probe into the thickest part of the rack of pork. On the off chance that your grill doesn't have meat probe capabilities or you don't claim a remote meat probe at that point, utilize a moment read computerized thermometer during the cook for internal temperature readings.
7. Place the rack rib-side down directly on the grill grates.
8. Smoke the rack of pork for 3 to 3½ hours, until the internal temperature arrives at 140°F.
9. Remove from the meat from the smoker, and let it rest under a free foil tent for 15 minutes before cutting.

Nutrition: Calories: 189 kCal Protein: 17 g Fat: 12 g

Tender Grilled Loin Chops

Preparation Time: 10 minutes

Cooking Time: 12 to 15 minutes

Servings: 6

Ingredients:

Traeger: Any

- 6 boneless focus cut midsection pork cleaves, 1 to 1½ inches thick 2 quarts Pork Brine
- 2 tablespoons roasted garlic–seasoned extra-virgin olive oil
- 2 teaspoons black pepper

Directions:

1. Trim abundance fat and silver skin from the pork slashes.
2. Place the pork slashes and brine in a 1-gallon sealable pack and refrigerate for in any event 12 hours or medium-term.
3. Remove the pork slashes from the brine and pat them dry with paper towels.
4. Brined pork hacks cook quicker than un-brined cleaves, so be mindful so as to screen internal temperatures.
5. Rest the pork slashes under a foil tent for 5 minutes before serving.

Nutrition: Calories: 211 kCal Protein: 17 g Fat: 21 g

Florentine Ribeye Pork Loin

Preparation Time: 30 minutes

Cooking Time: 60 to 75 minutes

Servings: 6 to 8

Ingredients:

- 1 (3-pound) boneless ribeye pork loin roast
- 4 tablespoons extra-virgin olive oil, divided
- 2 tablespoons Pork Dry Rub or your favorite pork seasoning
- 4 bacon slices
- 6 cups fresh spinach
- 1 small red onion, diced
- 6 cloves garlic, cut into thin slivers
- ¾ cup shredded mozzarella cheese

Directions:

1. Trim away any abundance fat and silver skin.
2. Butterfly the pork loin or approach your butcher to butterfly it for you. There are numerous phenomenal recordings online with nitty gritty directions on the various systems for butterflying a loin roast.
3. Rub 2 tablespoons of the olive oil on each side of the butterflied roast and season the two sides with the rub.
4. Cook the bacon in a large skillet over medium heat. Disintegrate and set aside. Reserve the bacon fat.
5. Grill the pork loin for 60 to 75 minutes, or until the internal temperature at the thickest part arrives at 140°F.
6. Rest the pork loin under a free foil tent for 15 minutes before cutting contrary to what would be expected.

Nutrition: Calories: 365 kCal Protein: 32.1 g Fat: 22 g

Naked St. Louis Ribs

Preparation Time: 30 minutes

Cooking Time: 5 to 6 hours

Servings: 6 to 8

Ingredients:

Traeger: Hickory, Apple

- 3 St. Louis–style pork rib racks
- 1 cup in addition to 1 tablespoon Jan's Original Dry Rub or your preferred pork rub

Directions:

1. Remove the membrane on the underside of the rib racks by embedding a spoon handle between the membrane and rib bones. Get the membrane with a paper towel and gradually dismantle it down the rack to remove.
2. Rub the two sides of the ribs with a liberal measure of the rub.
3. Arrange the traeger smoker-grill for a non-direct cooking and preheat to 225°F utilizing hickory or apple traegers.
4. In the event of utilizing a rib rack, place the ribs in the rack on the grill grates. Else you can utilize Teflon-covered fiberglass tangles or place the ribs directly on the grill grates.
5. Smoke the ribs at 225°F for 5 to 6 hours with hickory traegers until the internal temperature, at the thickest part of the ribs, arrives at 185°F to190°F.
6. Rest the ribs under a free foil tent for 10 minutes before cutting and serving.

Nutrition: Calories: 241kCal Protein: 23.6 g Fat: 13 g

GRILL LAMB RECIPES

Traeger Smoked Pulled Lamb Sliders

Preparation Time: 10 Minutes

Cooking Time: 9 Hours

Servings: 7

Ingredients:

- 5 lb. lamb shoulder, boneless
- 1/2 cup olive oil
- 1/3 cup kosher salt
- 1/3 cup pepper, coarsely ground
- 1/3 cup granulated garlic

For the spritz

- 4 oz Worcestershire sauce
- 6 oz apple cider vinegar

Directions:

1. Preheat the Traeger to 2250F with a pan of water for moisture.
2. Trim any excess fat from the lamb, then pat it dry with some paper towel. Rub with oil, salt, pepper, and garlic.
3. Place the lamb in the Traeger smoker for 90 minutes, then spritz every 30 minutes until the internal temperature reaches 1650F.
4. Transfer the lamb to a foil pan, then add the remaining spritz liquid. Cover with a foil and place back in the Traeger.
5. Smoke until the internal temperature reaches 2050F.
6. Remove from the smoker and let rest in a cooler without ice for 30 minutes before pulling it.
7. Serve with slaw or bun and enjoy.

Nutrition: Calories 235 Total Fat 6g Total Carbs 22g Protein 20g Sugars 7g Fiber 1g Sodium 592mg Potassium 318mg

Traeger Smoked Lamb Meatballs

Preparation Time: 10 Minutes

Cooking Time: 1 Hour

Servings: 20 Meatballs

Ingredients:

- 1 lb. lamb shoulder, ground
- Three garlic cloves, finely diced
- 3 tbsp. shallot, diced
- 1 tbsp. salt
- One egg
- 1/2 tbsp. pepper
- 1/2 tbsp. cumin
- 1/2 tbsp. smoked paprika
- 1/4 tbsp. red pepper flakes
- 1/4 tbsp. cinnamon
- 1/4 cup panko breadcrumbs

Directions:

1. Set your Traeger to 2500F.
2. Combine all the fixings in a small bowl, then mix thoroughly using your hands.
3. Form golf ball-sized meatballs and place them on a baking sheet.
4. Place the baking sheet in the smoker and smoke until the internal temperature reaches 1600F.
5. Remove the meatballs from the smoker and serve when hot.

Nutrition: Calories 93 Total fat 5.9g Total carbs 4.8g Protein 5gSugars 0.3gFiber 0.3gSodium 174.1mg Potassium 82.8mg

Traeger Crown Rack of Lamb

Preparation Time: 30 Minutes

Cooking Time: 30 Minutes

Servings: 6

Ingredients:

- Two racks of lamb. Frenched
- 1 tbsp garlic, crushed
- 1 tbsp rosemary
- 1/2 cup olive oil
- Kitchen twine

Directions:

1. Preheat your Traeger to 4500F.
2. Rinse the lab with clean cold water, then pat it dry with a paper towel.
3. Lay the lamb even on a chopping board and score a ¼ inch down between the bones. Repeat the process between the bones on each lamb rack. Set aside.
4. In a small mixing bowl, combine garlic, rosemary, and oil. Brush the lamb rack generously with the mixture.
5. Bend the lamb rack into a semicircle, then place the racks together such that the bones will be up and will form a crown shape.
6. Wrap around four times, starting from the base moving upward. Tie tightly to keep the racks together.
7. Place the lambs on a baking sheet and set in the Traeger. Cook on high heat for 10 minutes. Reduce the temperature to 3000F and cook for 20 more minutes or until the internal temperature reaches 1300F.
8. Remove the lamb rack from the Traeger and let rest while wrapped in a foil for 15 minutes.
9. Serve when hot.

Nutrition: Calories 390 Total fat 35g Total carbs 0g Protein 17g Sodium 65mg

Traeger Smoked Leg

Preparation Time: 15 Minutes

Cooking Time: 3 Hours

Servings: 6

Ingredients:

- One leg of lamb, boneless
- 2 tbsp oil
- Four garlic cloves, minced
- 2 tbsp oregano
- 1 tbsp thyme
- 2 tbsp salt
- 1 tbsp black pepper, freshly ground

Directions:

1. Trim excess fat from the lamb, ensuring you keep the meat in an even thickness for even cooking.
2. In a mixing bowl, mix oil, garlic, and all spices. Rub the mixture all over the lamb, then cover with a plastic wrap.
3. Place the lamb in a fridge and let marinate for an hour.
4. Transfer the lamb on a smoker rack and set the Traeger to smoke at 2500F.
5. Smoke the meat for 4 hours or until the internal temperature reaches 1450F
6. Remove from the Traeger and serve immediately.

Nutrition: Calories 356 Total fat 16g Total carbs 3g Protein 49gSugars 1gFiber 1gSodium 2474mg

GRILL POULTRY RECIPES

Traditional Thanksgiving Turkey

Preparation Time: 30 minutes

Cooking Time: 1 hour 30 minutes

Servings: 2-4

Ingredients:

- 1 (18-20lb) Turkey
- 1/2 Lb. Butter, Softened
- 8 Sprigs Thyme
- 6 Cloves Garlic, Minced
- 1 Sprig Rosemary, Rough Chop

Directions:

1. In a small bowl, combine butter with the minced garlic, thyme leaves, chopped rosemary, black pepper and kosher salt.
2. Prepare the turkey by separating the skin from the breast creating a pocket to stuff the butter-herb mixture in.
3. Cover the entire breast with 1/4" thickness of butter mixture.
4. Season the whole turkey with kosher salt and black pepper. As an option, you can also stuff the turkey cavity with Traditional Stuffing.
5. When ready to cook, set the temperature to 300 F and preheat, lid closed for 15 minutes.

Nutrition: Calories 956, Total fat 47g, Saturated fat 13g, Total carbs 1g, Net carbs 1g Protein 124g, Sugars 0g, Fiber 0g, Sodium 1750mg

Turkey Jalapeno Meatballs

Preparation Time: 30 minutes

Cooking Time: 1 hour 30 minutes

Servings: 2-4

Ingredients:

- Turkey Jalapeño Meatballs
- 1 1/4 Lbs. Ground Turkey
- 1 Jalapeño Pepper, Deseeded and Finely Diced
- 1/2 Tsp Garlic Salt
- 1 Tsp Onion Powder

Directions:

1. In a separate small bowl, combine the milk and bread crumbs.
2. In a large bowl, mix together turkey, garlic salt, onion powder, salt, pepper, Worcestershire sauce, cayenne pepper, egg and jalapeños.
3. Add the bread crumb milk mixture to the bowl and combine. Cover with plastic and refrigerate for up to 1 hour.
4. When ready to cook, set the temperature to 350°F and preheat, lid closed for 15 minutes
5. Roll the turkey mixture into balls, about one tablespoon each and place the meatballs in a single layer on a parchment lined baking sheet.

Nutrition: Calories 956, Total fat 47g, Saturated fat 13g, Total carbs 1g, Net carbs 1g Protein 124g, Sugars 0g, Fiber 0g, Sodium 2750mg

Wild Turkey Southwest Egg Rolls

Preparation Time: 30 minutes

Cooking Time: 1 hour 30 minutes

Servings: 2-4

Ingredients:

- 2 Cups Leftover Wild Turkey Meat
- 1/2 Cup Corn
- 1/2 Cup Black Beans
- 3 Tbsp Taco Seasoning
- 1/2 Cup White Onion, Chopped

Directions:

1. Add olive oil to a large skillet and heat on the stove over medium heat. Add onions and peppers and sauté 2-3 minutes until soft. Add garlic, cook 30 seconds, then Rote and black beans.
2. Pour taco seasoning over meat and add 1/3 cup of water and mix to coat well. Add to veggie mixture and stir to mix well. If it seems dry, add 2 tbsp water. Cook until heated all the way through.
3. Remove from the heat and transfer the mixture to the fridge. The mixture should be completely cooled prior to stuffing the egg rolls or the wrappers will break.
4. Place spoonful of the mixture in each wrapper and wrap tightly. Repeat with remaining wrappers. When ready to cook, set temperature to High and preheat, lid closed for 15 minutes.
5. Brush each egg roll with oil or butter and place directly on the Traeger grill grate. Cook until the exterior is crispy, about 20 min per side.

Nutrition: Calories 456, Total fat 37g, Saturated fat 13g, Total carbs 1g, Net carbs 1g Protein 124g, Sugars 0g, Fiber 0g, Sodium 1750mg

Smoked Wild Turkey Breast

Preparation Time: 30 minutes

Cooking Time: 1 hour 30 minutes

Servings: 2-4

Ingredients:

- Brine
- 2 Lbs. Turkey Breast and Deboned Thigh, Tied with Skin On
- 1 Cup Brown Sugar
- 1/4 Cup Salt
- 2 Tbsp Cracked Pepper
- 4 Cups Cold Water
- BBQ Rub
- 2 Tbsp Garlic Powder
- 2 Tbsp Onions, Dried
- 2 Tbsp Black Pepper
- 2 Tbsp Brown Sugar
- 1 Tbsp Cayenne Pepper
- 2 Tbsp Chili Powder
- 1/4 Cup Paprika
- 1 Tbsp Salt
- 2 Tbsp Sugar
- 2 Tbsp Cumin, Ground

Directions:

1. For the Brine: In a large glass bowl combine brown sugar, salt, pepper and water. Add turkey and weigh down to completely submerge if necessary. Transfer to the refrigerator and brine.
2. Remove turkey from the brine and discard the brine.
3. When ready to cook, set the temperature 180 F and preheat lid closed for 15 minutes.
4. Combine Ingredients for the BBQ Rub. Season turkey with rub and place directly on the grill grate skin side up.
5. Smoke for 5-8 hours or until the internal temperature reaches 160 F degrees when an instant read thermometer is inserted into the center.
6. Remove from the smoker and let rest for 10 minutes. Turkey will continue to cook once taken off grill to reach a final temperature of 165 F in the breast.
7. Slice and serve with your favorite sides. Enjoy!

Nutrition: Calories 856, Total fat 47g, Saturated fat 13g, Total carbs 2g, Net carbs 1g Protein 124g, Sugars 0g, Fiber 0g, Sodium 1750mg

Grilled Wild Turkey Orange Cashew Salad

Preparation Time: 30 minutes

Cooking Time: 1 hour 30 minutes

Servings: 2-4

Ingredients:

- Turkey Breast
- 2 Wild Turkey Breast Halves, Without Skin
- 1/4 Cup Teriyaki Sauce
- 1 Tsp Fresh Ginger
- 1 (12 Oz) Can Blood Orange Kill Cliff or Similar Citrus Soda
- 2 Tbsp Traeger Chicken Rub
- Cashew Salad
- 4 Cups Romaine Lettuce, Chopped
- 1/2 Head Red or White Cabbage, Chopped
- 1/2 Cup Shredded Carrots
- 1/2 Cup Edamame, Shelled
- 1 Smoked Yellow Bell Pepper, Sliced into Circles
- 1 Smoked Red Bell Pepper, Sliced into Circles
- 3 Chive Tips, Chopped
- 1/2 Cup Smoked Cashews
- Blood Orange Vinaigrette
- 1 Tsp Orange Zest
- Juice From 1/2 Large Orange
- 1 Tsp Finely Grated Fresh Ginger
- 2 Tbsp Seasoned Rice Vinegar
- 1 Tsp Honey
- Sea Salt, To Taste
- 1/4 Cup Light Vegetable Oil

Directions:

1. For the Marinade: Combine teriyaki sauce, Kill Cliff soda and fresh ginger. Pour marinade over turkey breasts in a Ziplock bag or dish and seal.
2. When ready to cook, set temperature to 375 F and preheat, lid closed for 15 minutes.
3. Remove turkey from the refrigerator, drain the marinade and pat turkey dry with paper towels.
4. Place turkey into a shallow oven proof dish and season with Traeger Chicken Rub.
5. Place dish in the Traeger and cook for 30-45 minutes or until the breast reaches an internal temperature of 160 F.
6. Remove the breast from the grill and wrap in Traeger Butcher Paper. Let turkey rest for 10 minutes. While turkey is resting, prepare salad.
7. Assemble salad Ingredients in a bowl and toss to mix. Combine all Ingredients in list for vinaigrette.
8. After resting for 10 minutes, slice turkey and serve with cashew salad and blood orange vinaigrette. Enjoy!

Nutrition: Calories 956, Total fat 47g, Saturated fat 13g, Total carbs 1g, Net carbs 1g Protein 124g, Sugars 0g, Fiber 0g, Sodium 1750mg

Baked Cornbread Turkey Tamale Pie

Preparation Time: 30 minutes

Cooking Time: 1 hour 30 minutes

Servings: 2-4

Ingredients:

- Filling
- 2 Cups Shredded Turkey
- 2 Cobs of Corn
- 1 (15 Oz) Can Black Beans, Rinsed and Drained
- 1 Yellow Bell Pepper
- 1 Orange Bell Pepper
- 2 Jalapeños
- 2 Tbsp Cilantro
- 1 Bunch Green Onions
- 1/2 Tsp Cumin
- 1/2 Tsp Paprika
- 1 (7 Oz) Can Chipotle Sauce
- 1 (15 Oz) Can Enchilada Sauce
- 1/2 Cup Shredded Cheddar Cheese
- Cornbread Topping
- 1 Cup All-Purpose Flour
- 1 Cup Yellow or White Cornmeal
- 1 Tbsp Sugar
- 2 Tsp Baking Powder
- 1/2 Tsp Salt
- 3 Tbsp Butter
- 1 Cup Buttermilk
- 1 Large Egg, Lightly Beaten

Directions:

1. For the filling: Mix to combine filling Ingredients Place in the bottom of a butter greased 10-inch pan.
2. For the cornbread topping: In a mixing bowl, combine the flour, cornmeal, sugar, baking powder, and salt. Melt the butter in a small saucepan.
3. Add the milk-egg mixture to the dry Ingredients and stir to combine. Do not over mix.
4. To assemble Tamale Pie: Fill the bottom of a butter greased 10-inch pan with the shredded turkey filling. Top with the cornbread topping and smooth to the edges of pan.
5. When ready to cook, set the temperature to 375 F and preheat, lid closed for 15 minutes.
6. Place directly on the grill grate and cook for 45-50 minutes or until the cornbread is lightly browned and cooked through. Enjoy!

Nutrition: Calories 956, Total fat 47g, Saturated fat 13g, Total carbs 1g, Net carbs 1g Protein 124g, Sugars 0g, Fiber 0g, Sodium 1750mg

TURKEY, RABBIT AND VEAL

Smoke Roasted Chicken

Preparation Time: 20 minutes

Cooking Time: 1 hour 20 minutes

Servings: 4-6

Ingredients:

- 8 tablespoon butter, room temperature
- 1 clove garlic, minced
- 1 scallion, minced
- 2 tablespoon fresh herbs such as thyme, rosemary, sage or parsley
- As needed Chicken rub
- Lemon juice
- As needed vegetable oil

Directions:

1. In a small cooking bowl, mix the scallions, garlic, butter, minced fresh herbs, 1-1/2 teaspoon of the rub, and lemon juice. Mix with a spoon.
2. Remove any giblets from the cavity of the chicken. Wash the chicken inside and out with cold running water. Dry thoroughly with paper towels.
3. Sprinkle a generous amount of Chicken Rub inside the cavity of the chicken.
4. Gently loosen the skin around the chicken breast and slide in a few tablespoons of the herb butter under the skin and cover.
5. Cover the outside with the remaining herb butter.
6. Insert the chicken wings behind the back. Tie both legs together with a butcher's string.
7. Powder the outside of the chicken with more Chicken Rub then insert sprigs of fresh herbs inside the cavity of the chicken.
8. Set temperature to High and preheat, lid closed for 15 minutes.
9. Oil the grill with vegetable oil. Move the chicken on the grill grate, breast-side up then close the lid.
10. After chicken has cooked for 1 hour, lift the lid. If chicken is browning too quickly, cover the breast and legs with aluminum foil.
11. Close the lid then continue to roast the chicken until an instant-read meat thermometer inserted into the thickest part registers a temperature of 165F
12. Take off chicken from grill and let rest for 5 minutes. Serve, Enjoy!

Nutrition: Calories 222kcal Carbohydrates 11g Protein 29g Fat 4g Cholesterol 62mg Sodium 616mg Potassium 620mg

Grilled Asian Chicken Burgers

Preparation Time: 5 minutes

Cooking Time: 50 minutes

Servings: 4-6

Ingredients:

- Pound chicken, ground
- 1 cup panko breadcrumbs
- 1 cup parmesan cheese
- 1 small jalapeno, diced
- 2 whole scallions, minced
- 2 garlic clove
- ¼ cup minced cilantro leaves
- 2 tablespoon mayonnaise
- 2 tablespoon chili sauce
- 1 tablespoon soy sauce
- 1 tablespoon ginger, minced
- 2 teaspoon lemon juice
- 2 teaspoon lemon zest
- 1 teaspoon salt
- 1 teaspoon ground black pepper
- 8 hamburger buns
- 1 tomato, sliced
- Arugula, fresh
- 1 red onion sliced

Directions:

1. Align a rimmed baking sheet with aluminum foil then spray with nonstick cooking spray.
2. In a large bowl, combine the chicken, jalapeno, scallion, garlic, cilantro, panko, Parmesan, chili sauce, soy sauce ginger, mayonnaise, lemon juice and zest, and salt and pepper.
3. Work the mixture with your fingers until the ingredients are well combined. If the mixture looks too wet to form patties and add additional more panko.
4. Wash your hands under cold running water, form the meat into 8 patties, each about an inch larger than the buns and about ¾" thick. Use your thumbs or a tablespoon, make a wide, shallow depression in the top of each
5. Put them on the prepared baking sheet. Spray the tops with nonstick cooking spray. If not cooking right away, cover with plastic wrap and refrigerate.
6. Set the traeger grill to 350F then preheat for 15 minutes, lid closed.
7. Order the burgers, depression-side down, on the grill grate. Remove and discard the foil on the baking sheet so you'll have an uncontaminated surface to transfer the slider when cooked.
8. Grill the burgers for about 25 to 30 minutes, turning once, or until they release easily from the grill grate when a clean metal spatula is slipped under them. The internal temperature when read on an instant-read meat thermometer should be 160F.

9. Spread mayonnaise and arrange a tomato slice, if desired, and a few arugula leaves on one-half of each bun. Top with a grilled burger and red onions, if using, then replace the top half of the bun. Serve immediately. Enjoy

Nutrition: Calories 329kcal Carbohydrates 10g Protein 21g Fat 23g

Grilled Sweet Cajun Wings

Preparation Time: 10 minutes

Cooking Time: 45 minutes

Servings: 4-6

Ingredients:

- 2-pound chicken wings
- As needed Pork and Poultry rub
- Cajun shake

Directions:

1. Coat wings in Sweet rub and Cajun shake.
2. When ready to cook, set the traeger grill to 350F and preheat, lid closed for 15 minutes.
3. Cook for 30 minutes until skin is brown and center is juicy and an instant-read thermometer reads at least 165F. Serve, Enjoy!

The Grilled Chicken Challenge

Preparation Time: 15 minutes

Cooking Time: 1 hour and 10 minutes

Servings: 4-6

Ingredients:

- 1 (4-lbs.) whole chicken
- As needed chicken rub

Directions:

1. When ready to cook, set temperature to 375F then preheat, close the lid for 15 minutes.
2. Rinse and dry the whole chicken (remove and discard giblets, if any). Season the entire chicken, including the inside of the chicken using chicken rub.
3. Place the chicken on the grill and cook for 1 hour and 10 minutes.
4. Remove chicken from grill when internal temperature of breast reaches 160F. Check heat periodically throughout as cook times will vary based on the weight of the chicken.
5. Allow chicken to rest until the internal temperature of breast reaches 165F, 15-20 minutes. Enjoy!

Nutrition: Calories 212kcal Carbohydrates 42.6g Protein 6.1g Fat 2.4g Saturated Fat 0.5g Fiber 3.4g Sugar 2.9g

Chicken Breast with Lemon

Preparation Time: 15min

Cooking Time: 15min

Servings: 6

Ingredients:

- 6 Chicken breasts, skinless and boneless
- ½ cup Oil
- 1 - 2 Fresh thyme sprigs
- 1 tsp. ground black pepper
- 2 tsp. Salt
- 2 tsp. of Honey
- 1 Garlic clove, chopped
- 1 Lemon the juice and zest
- For service: Lemon wedges

Directions:

1. In a bowl combine the thyme, black pepper, salt, honey, garlic, and lemon zest and juice. Stir until dissolved and combined. Add the oil and whisk to combine.
2. Clean the breasts and pat dry. Place them in a plastic bag. Pour the pre-made marinade and massage to distribute evenly. Place in the fridge, 4 hours.
3. Preheat the grill to 400F with the lid closed.
4. Drain the chicken and grill until the internal temperature reaches 165F, about 15 minutes.
5. Serve with lemon wedges and a side dish of your choice.

Nutrition: Calories: 230 Proteins: 38g Carbohydrates: 1g Fat: 7g

Traeger Smoked Chicken Burgers

Preparation Time: 20 minutes

Cooking Time: 1 hour and 10 minutes

Servings: 6

Ingredients:

- 2 lb. ground chicken breast
- 2/3 cup of finely chopped onions
- 1 Tbsps. of cilantro, finely chopped
- 2 Tbsp. fresh parsley, finely chopped
- 2 Tbsp. of olive oil
- 1/2 tsp of ground cumin
- 2 Tbsps. of lemon juice freshly squeezed
- 3/4 tsp of salt and red pepper to taste

Directions:

1. In a bowl add all ingredients; mix until combined well.
2. Form the mixture into 6 patties.
3. Start your traeger grill on SMOKE (oak or apple traegers) with the lid open until the fire is established. Set the heat to 350F and preheat, lid closed, for 10 to 15 minutes.
4. Smoke the chicken burgers for 45 - 50 minutes or until cooked through, turning every 15 minutes.
5. Your burgers are ready when internal temperature reaches 165 F
6. Serve hot.

Nutrition: Calories: 221 Carbohydrates: 2.12g Fat: 8.5g Fiber: 0.4g Protein: 32.5g

Perfect Smoked Chicken Patties

Preparation Time: 20 minutes

Cooking Time: 50 minutes

Servings: 6

Ingredients:

- 2 lb. ground chicken breast
- 2/3 cup minced onion
- 1 Tbsps. cilantro (chopped)
- 2 Tbsp. fresh parsley, finely chopped
- 2 Tbsp. olive oil
- 1/8 tsp crushed red pepper flakes
- 1/2 tsp ground cumin
- 2 Tbsps. fresh lemon juice
- 3/4 tsp kosher salt
- 2 tsp paprika
- Hamburger buns for serving

Directions:

1. In a bowl combine all ingredients from the list.
2. Using your hands, mix well. Form mixture into 6 patties. Refrigerate until ready to grill (about 30 minutes).
3. Start your traeger grill on SMOKE with the lid open until the fire is established). Set the temperature to 350F and preheat for 10 to 15 minutes.
4. Arrange chicken patties on the grill rack and cook for 35 to 40 minutes turning once.
5. Serve hot with hamburger buns and your favorite condiments.

Nutrition: Calories: 258 Carbohydrates: 2.5g Fat: 9.4g Fiber: 0.6g Protein: 39g

SMOKING RECIPES

Smoked Apple Pork Butt Recipe

Preparation Time: 10 minutes

Cooking Time: 4-6 hours

Servings: 7

Ingredients:

- 1 1/2 cups brown sugar
- 1/2 cup kosher salt
- 1/3 cup ground black pepper
- 1/4 cup ground paprika
- 1/4 cup garlic powder
- 1/4 cup Italian seasoning
- 2 tbsp. onion powder
- 2 tbsp. chili powder
- 2 tbsp. cayenne pepper
- 1 tbsp. ground cumin
- 1 tsp. dried sage
- 1/2 cup apple cider
- 1/4 cup apple juice concentrate
- 2 tbsp. honey
- 2 tbsp. Worcestershire sauce
- 3 drops liquid smoke flavoring
- 7 pounds bone-in pork butt
- 1/2 cup yellow mustard
- 1 tbsp. honey
- 1 cup of whiskey barrel wood chips (such as jack Daniel's)
- 1/2 cup applewood chips
- 1/2 cup apple juice concentrate
- 1/2 cup water

Directions

1. Combine brown sugar, salt, pepper, paprika, garlic, Italian seasoning, onion powder, chili powder, cayenne pepper, cumin, and sage in a little container—measure one tablespoon of the dry rub mixture into a huge box that may fit the pork butt. Refrigerate the remaining dry rub.
2. Mix the apple cider, 1/4 cup apple juice concentrate, two tablespoons honey, Worcestershire sauce, and liquid smoke into the large container to create the marinade.

3. String the top of the pork butt in a checkerboard pattern. Inject a few of the marinade into the bottom, sides, and the surface of the pork butt—place pork in the jar with the remaining marinade. Put the marinate in the refrigerator, 8 hours to overnight.
4. Combine whiskey barrel wood chips, applewood chips, 1/2 cup apple juice concentrate, and water in a sizable resealable bag. Seal and let soak, about 20 minutes.
5. Turn heat an electric smoker to 225 degrees F (110 degrees C). Fill the smoker box with wood chips according to the manufacturer's instructions.
6. Remove pork from marinade; rub mustard and one tablespoon honey evenly at the top. Coat pork butts heavily with dry rub—place fat-side through to a rack.
7. Put the shelf in the smoker; Cook until the center inserted instant thermometer reads 160 ° F (71 ° C) to an average or 170 ° F (77 ° C), 4 to 6 hours. Add more soaked wood chips midway through the cooking period. Place pork butt fat-side through to a sizable platter. Let rest for 20 minutes then cover it with aluminum foil and, turning over halfway through resting time.

Nutrition: Energy (calories): 1535 kcal Protein: 117.27 g Fat: 82.29 g Carbohydrates: 77.74 g

Smoked Beer-Can Turkey Recipe

Preparation Time: 30 minutes

Cooking Time: 2-3 hours

Servings: 8

Ingredients

For the brine

- 2 quarts apple juice
- 1 cup kosher salt
- 1/2 cup brown sugar
- 1/4 cup molasses
- 3 quarts ice cold water
- One whole natural turkey, 12 to 14 pounds

For the rub

- 1 tbsp. paprika
- 1 tsp. kosher salt
- 1 tsp. chili powder
- 1 tsp. garlic powder
- 1 tsp. freshly ground black pepper
- 1/2 teaspoon onion powder
- 1/2 teaspoon dried thyme
- 1/2 teaspoon dried oregano
- 1/4 teaspoon ground cumin
- 1/4 teaspoon cayenne pepper

One medium chunk of applewood or other light smoking wood

- 1 (24 ounces) tall can of beer

Type of fire: indirect

Grill heat: medium

Directions

To make the brine:

1. Whisk together the apple juice, salt, brown sugar and molasses in a large container until the salt and sugar have dissolved. Mix 3 liters of ice cold water. Dip the turkey, breast side down, into the brine. Put the container in the refrigerator and salt for 12 hours. To help make the rub: In a little bowl, combine paprika, salt, chili powder, garlic powder, black pepper, onion powder, thyme, oregano, cumin, and cayenne pepper. Reserve.
2. Remove the turkey from the brine. Dry inside and outside with paper towels. I use fingers to gently separate the skin from the flesh under the breasts and around the thighs. Spread about 1 1/2 tablespoons of rubbing under your chest and thighs. Sprinkle remaining friction around the turkey inside and out.

3. Turn up smoker or grill to 325degrees F, adding smoking wood chunks when at temperature. When the wood is ignited and generating smoke, drink or empty 1/3 of beer and place the smokers can. Carefully lower turkey onto beer can, legs down. Adjust turkey legs, so it stands vertical stably. Cover and smoke until an instant-read thermometer register 160degrees F in the breast's thickest portion, about 2-3 hours.
4. Take away the turkey from the smoker and invite to rest, uncovered, for 20 to 30 minutes. Remove beer can carve and serve.

Nutrition: Energy (calories): 325 kcal Protein: 9.61 g Fat: 21.98 g Carbohydrates: 22.51 g

Sweet Smoked Pork Ribs Recipe

Preparation Time: 30 minutes

Cooking Time: 3-4 hours

Servings: 10

Ingredients

- 1/4 cup salt
- 1/4 cup white sugar
- 2 tbsp. packed brown sugar
- 2 tbsp. ground black pepper
- 2 tbsp. ground white peppers
- 2 tbsp. onion powder
- 1 tbsp. garlic powder
- 1 tbsp. chili powder
- 1 tbsp. ground paprika
- 1 tbsp. ground cumin
- 10 pounds of baby back pork ribs
- 1 cup apple juice
- 1/4 cup packed brown sugar
- 1/4 cup barbeque sauces

Directions

1. Stir salt, white sugar, two tablespoons brown sugar, black pepper, white pepper, onion powder, garlic powder, chili powder, paprika, and cumin together in a little bowl to help make the dry rub. Rub the spice blend into the back ribs on all sides. Wrap the ribs generously with plastic wrap, and refrigerate for at least 30 minutes just before cooking.
2. Unwrap baby back ribs and place them onto the wire racks of the smoker within a layer.
3. Place the racks right into a smoker, fill the smoker pan with apple, grape, pear, or cherry chips, and bring the smoker to 270 degrees F (130 degrees C)—smoke for one hour.
4. Stir in the apple juice, 1/4 cup of brown sugar and barbecue sauce. Brush the ribs with the sauce every 30 to 45 minutes following the first hour. Cook the smoker's ribs before the meat is no longer pink and begins to "shrink" back from the bones, 3 to 4 hours. Brush the sauce onto the ribs one final time 30 minutes before the ribs will be ready to be taken from the smoker.
5. Once the ribs are done, wrap them tightly with aluminum foil, and invite them to rest 10 to a quarter-hour. It allows the juices to reabsorb into the meat and make the ribs moist.

Nutrition: Energy (calories): 869 kcal Protein: 95.47 g Fat: 26.98 g Carbohydrates: 56.95 g

Baked Green Bean Casserole

Preparation time: 10 minutes

Cooking time: 50 minutes

Servings: 12

Ingredients:

- 3 lbs. trimmed green beans - Kosher salt - 2 tbsps. olive oil
- 2 tbsps. unsalted butter - 1/2 lb. shitake or king trumpet mushrooms, sliced
- 1/4 cup minced shallot - 1/4 cup rice flour
- 2 cups chicken stock - 1/2 cup sherry cooking wine
- 1 cup heavy cream - 1 cup grated Parmigiano Reggiano
- 1 cup slivered almonds, for topping - 4 cups canola or vegetable oil
- Eight whole, peeled shallots - 1/2 cup rice flour - 1 tsp. kosher salt

Intolerances:

- Egg-Free

Directions:

1. Make the temperature to High and preheat, lid closed for 15 minutes.
2. Fill a large stockpot 2/3 full of water and bring to a boil over high heat. Prepare a large ice bath. If the water is already boiling, add 1 tbsp. of salt.
3. Once the water has come to a boil, add half the green beans. Cook until al dente, about 2 minutes. Remove with a colander and place the beans in the ice bath to cool.
4. Take the green beans out of the water and place them on paper towels to dry. Repeat with the rest of the green beans.

To make the Sauce:

1. Melt the butter and olive oil in a small saucepan over medium heat.
2. Add the shallots and mushrooms and a generous pinch of salt and cook, stirring, until the mushrooms are soft, about 5 minutes.
3. Sprinkle such rice flour over the top and then stir to coat the mushrooms, and cook off the raw flour taste, about 2 minutes.
4. Add some sherry, stir and reduce, then slowly stir in the stock, allowing thickening and ensuring there are no lumps, about 3 minutes.
5. Stir in the cream and Parmigiano-Reggiano. Taste, adding salt and pepper as needed.
6. Combine the green beans with the sauce. Then pour into a large oven-proof serving dish. Sprinkle with almonds.
7. Bake until the sauce is bubbling and the almonds are browned about 30 minutes.
8. The moment that the green beans are on the grill, fry the shallots. Put the oil in a deep saucepan or Dutch oven and heat oil to 350degrees F.
9. Put the rice flour and salt in a shallow bowl and mix with a fork. Cut the shallots into 1/8-inch rings. Mix the shallots to cover them with the rice flour, shaking them off in a colander. Fry the shallots in batches until golden brown, about 30 seconds to one minute. Drain on paper towels.
10. Prepare casserole and ready, garnish with the fried shallots. Enjoy!

Nutrition: Calories: 190 Fats: 10g Cholesterol: 1mg Carbs: 20g Protein: 5g

FISH AND SEAFOOD RECIPES

Roasted Yellowtail

Preparation Time: 10 minutes

Cooking Time: 30 minutes

Servings: 4

Ingredients:

- 4 Yellowtail Filets (6 oz.)
- 1 lb. new Potatoes
- 2 tbsp. Olive oil
- 1 lb. Mushrooms, oyster
- 1 tsp. ground Black pepper
- 4 tbsp. of olive oil

Salsa Verde:

- 1 tbsp. Cilantro, chopped
- 2 tbsp. Mint, chopped
- ½ cup Parsley, chopped
- 2 cloves of garlic, minced
- 1 tbsp. Oregano, chopped
- 1 Lemon, the juice
- 1 cup of Olive oil
- 1/8 tsp. Pepper Flake
- Salt

Directions:

1. Preheat the grill to high with closed lid.
2. Place an iron pan directly on the grill. Let it heat for 10 minutes.
3. Rub the fish with oil. Season with black pepper and salt.
4. In a 2 different bowls place the mushrooms and potatoes, drizzle with oil and season with black pepper and salt. Toss.
5. Place the potatoes in the pan. Cook 10 minutes. Add the mushrooms.
6. Place the fillets on the grate with the skin down. Cook for 6 minutes and flip. Cook for 4 minutes more.
7. While the potatoes, mushrooms, and fish are cooking make the Salsa Verde. In a bowl combine all the ingredients and stir to combine.
8. Place the mushrooms and potatoes on a plate, top with a fillet and drizzle with the Salsa Verde.
9. Serve and Enjoy!

Nutrition: Calories: 398 Protein: 52g Carbs: 20g Fat: 18gg

Baked Steelhead

Preparation Time: 15 minutes

Cooking Time: 20 minutes

Servings: 4 - 6

Ingredients:

- 1 Lemon
- 2 Garlic cloves, minced
- ½ Shallot, minced
- 3 tbsp. Butter, unsalted
- Saskatchewan seasoning, blackened
- Italian Dressing
- 1 Steelhead, (a fillet)

Directions:

1. Preheat the grill to 350F with closed lid.
2. In an iron pan place the butter. Place the pan in the grill while preheating so that the butter melts. Coat the fillet with Italian dressing. Rub with Saskatchewan rub. Make sure the layer is thin.
3. Mince the garlic and shallot. Remove the pan from the grill and add the garlic and shallots.
4. Spread the mixture on the fillet. Slice the lemon into slices. Place the slice on the butter mix.
5. Place the fish on the grate. Cook 20 - 30 minutes.
6. Remove from the grill and serve. Enjoy!

Nutrition: Calories: 230 Protein: 28g Carbs 2g: Fat: 14g

Wine Brined Salmon

Preparation Time: 15 minutes

Cooking Time: 5 hours

Servings: 4

Ingredients:

- 2 cups low-sodium soy sauce
- 1 cup dry white wine
- 1 cup water
- ½ teaspoon Tabasco sauce
- 1/3 cup sugar
- ¼ cup salt
- ½ teaspoon garlic powder
- ½ teaspoon onion powder
- Ground black pepper, as required
- 4 (6-ounce) salmon fillets

Directions:

1. In a large bowl, add all ingredients except salmon and stir until sugar is dissolved.
2. Add salmon fillets and coat with brine well.
3. Refrigerate, covered overnight.
4. Remove salmon from bowl and rinse under cold running water.
5. With paper towels, pat dry the salmon fillets.
6. Arrange a wire rack in a sheet pan.
7. Place the salmon fillets onto wire rack, skin side down and set aside to cool for about 1 hour.
8. Preheat the Z Grills Traeger Grill & Smoker on smoke setting to 165 degrees F, using charcoal.
9. Arrange the salmon fillets onto the grill, skin side down and cook for about 3-5 hours or until desired doneness.
10. Remove the salmon fillets from grill and serve hot.

Nutrition: Calories 379 Total Fat 10.5 g Saturated Fat 1.5 g Cholesterol 75 mg Sodium 14000 mg Total Carbs 26.8 g Fiber 0.1 g Sugar 25.3 g Protein 41.1 g

Citrus Salmon

Preparation Time: 15 minutes

Cooking Time: 30 minutes

Servings: 6

Ingredients:

- 2 (1-pound) salmon fillets
- Salt and ground black pepper, as required
- 1 tablespoon seafood seasoning
- 2 lemons, sliced
- 2 limes, sliced

Directions:

1. Preheat the Z Grills Traeger Grill & Smoker on grill setting to 225 degrees F.
2. Season the salmon fillets with salt, black pepper and seafood seasoning evenly.
3. Place the salmon fillets onto the grill and top each with lemon and lime slices evenly.
4. Cook for about 30 minutes.
5. Remove the salmon fillets from grill and serve hot.

Nutrition: Calories 327 Total Fat 19.8 g Saturated Fat 3.6 g Cholesterol 81 mg Sodium 237 mg Total Carbs 1 g Fiber 0.3 g Sugar 0.2 g Protein 36.1 g

Simple Mahi-Mahi

Preparation Time: 10 minutes

Cooking Time: 10 minutes

Servings: 4

Ingredients:

- 4 (6-ounce) mahi-mahi fillets
- 2 tablespoons olive oil
- Salt and ground black pepper, as required

Directions:

1. Preheat the Z Grills Traeger Grill & Smoker on grill setting to 350 degrees F.
2. Coat fish fillets with olive oil and season with salt and black pepper evenly.
3. Place the fish fillets onto the grill and cook for about 5 minutes per side.
4. Remove the fish fillets from grill and serve hot.

Nutrition: Calories 195 Total Fat 7 g Saturated Fat 1 g Cholesterol 60 mg Sodium 182 mg Total Carbs 0 g Fiber 0 g Sugar 0 g Protein 31.6g

Rosemary Trout

Preparation Time: 10 minutes

Cooking Time: 5 hours

Servings: 8

Ingredients:

- 1 (7-pound) whole lake trout, butterflied
- ½ cup kosher salt
- ½ cup fresh rosemary, chopped
- 2 teaspoons lemon zest, grated finely

Directions:

1. Rub the trout with salt generously and then, sprinkle with rosemary and lemon zest.
2. Arrange the trout in a large baking dish and refrigerate for about 7-8 hours.
3. Remove the trout from baking dish and rinse under cold running water to remove the salt.
4. With paper towels, pat dry the trout completely.
5. Arrange a wire rack in a sheet pan.
6. Place the trout onto the wire rack, skin side down and refrigerate for about 24 hours.
7. Preheat the Z Grills Traeger Grill & Smoker on grill setting to 180 degrees F, using charcoal.
8. Place the trout onto the grill and cook for about 2-4 hours or until desired doneness.
9. Remove the trout from grill and place onto a cutting board for about 5 minutes before serving.

Nutrition: Calories 633 Total Fat 31.8 g Saturated Fat 7.9 g Cholesterol 153 mg Sodium 5000 mg Total Carbs 2.4 g Fiber 1.6 g Sugar 0 g Protein 85.2 g

Sesame Seeds Flounder

Preparation Time: 15 minutes

Cooking Time: 2½ hours

Servings: 4

Ingredients:

- ½ cup sesame seeds, toasted
- ½ teaspoon kosher salt flakes
- 1 tablespoon canola oil
- 1 teaspoon sesame oil
- 4 (6-ounce) flounder fillets

Directions:

1. Preheat the Z Grills Traeger Grill & Smoker on grill setting to 225 degrees F.
2. With a mortar and pestle, crush sesame seeds with kosher salt slightly.
3. In a small bowl, mix together both oils.
4. Coat fish fillets with oil mixture generously and then, rub with sesame seeds mixture.
5. Place fish fillets onto the lower rack of grill and cook for about 2-2½ hours.
6. Remove the fish fillets from grill and serve hot.

Nutrition: Calories 343 Total Fat 16.2 g Saturated Fat 2.3 g Cholesterol 116 mg Sodium 476 mg Total Carbs 4.2 g Fiber 2.1 g Sugar 0.1 g Protein 44.3 g

Parsley Prawn Skewers

Preparation Time: 15 minutes

Cooking Time: 8 minutes

Servings: 5

Ingredients:

- ¼ cup fresh parsley leaves, minced
- 1 tablespoon garlic, crushed
- 2½ tablespoons olive oil
- 2 tablespoons Thai chili sauce
- 1 tablespoon fresh lime juice
- 1½ pounds prawns, peeled and deveined

Directions:

1. In a large bowl, add all ingredients except for prawns and mix well.
2. In a resealable plastic bag, add marinade and prawns.
3. Seal the bag and shake to coat well
4. Refrigerate for about 20-30 minutes.
5. Preheat the Z Grills Traeger Grill & Smoker on grill setting to 450 degrees F.
6. Remove the prawns from marinade and thread onto metal skewers.
7. Arrange the skewers onto the grill and cook for about 4 minutes per side.
8. Remove the skewers from grill and serve hot.

Nutrition: Calories 234 Total Fat 9.3 g Saturated Fat 1.7 g Cholesterol 287 mg Sodium 562 mg Total Carbs 4.9 g Fiber 0.1 g Sugar 1.7 g Protein 31.2 g

Buttered Shrimp

Preparation Time: 15 minutes

Cooking Time: 30 minutes

Servings: 6

Ingredients:

- 8 ounces salted butter, melted
- ¼ cup Worcestershire sauce
- ¼ cup fresh parsley, chopped
- 1 lemon, quartered
- 2 pounds jumbo shrimp, peeled and deveined
- 3 tablespoons BBQ rub

Directions:

1. In a metal baking pan, add all ingredients except for shrimp and BBQ rub and mix well.
2. Season the shrimp with BBQ rub evenly.
3. Add shrimp in the pan with butter mixture and coat well.
4. Set aside for about 20-30 minutes.
5. Preheat the Z Grills Traeger Grill & Smoker on grill setting to 250 degrees F.
6. Place the pan onto the grill and cook for about 25-30 minutes.
7. Remove the pan from grill and serve hot.

Nutrition: Calories 462 Total Fat 33.3 g Saturated Fat 20.2 g Cholesterol 400 mg Sodium 485 mg Total Carbs 4.7 g Fiber 0.2 g Sugar 2.1 g Protein 34.9 g

Prosciutto Wrapped Scallops

Preparation Time: 15 minutes

Cooking Time: 40 minutes

Servings: 4

Ingredients:

- 8 large scallops, shelled and cleaned
- 8 extra-thin prosciutto slices

Directions:

1. Preheat the Z Grills Traeger Grill & Smoker on grill setting to 225-250 degrees F.
2. Arrange the prosciutto slices onto a smooth surface.
3. Place 1 scallop on the edge of 1 prosciutto slice and roll it up tucking in the sides of the prosciutto to cover completely.
4. Repeat with remaining scallops and prosciutto slices
5. Arrange the wrapped scallops onto a small wire rack.
6. Place the wire rack onto the grill and cook for about 40 minutes.
7. Remove the scallops from grill and serve hot.

Nutrition: Calories 160 Total Fat 6.7 g Saturated Fat 2.3 g Cholesterol 64 mg Sodium 1000 mg Total Carbs 1.4 g Fiber 0 g Sugar 0 g Protein 23.5 g

Buttered Clams

Preparation Time: 15 minutes

Cooking Time: 8 minutes

Servings: 6

Ingredients:

- 24 littleneck clams
- ½ cup cold butter, chopped
- 2 tablespoons fresh parsley, minced
- 3 garlic cloves, minced
- 1 teaspoon fresh lemon juice

Directions:

1. Preheat the Z Grills Traeger Grill & Smoker on grill setting to 450 degrees F.
2. Scrub the clams under cold running water.
3. In a large casserole dish, mix together remaining ingredients.
4. Place the casserole dish onto the grill.
5. Now, arrange the clams directly onto the grill and cook for about 5-8 minutes or until they are opened. (Discard any that fail to open).
6. With tongs, carefully transfer the opened clams into the casserole dish and remove from the grill.
7. Serve immediately.

Nutrition: Calories 306 Total Fat 17.6 g Saturated Fat 9.9 g Cholesterol 118 mg Sodium 237 mg Total Carbs 6.4 g Fiber 0.1 g Sugar 0.1 g Protein 29.3 g

VEGETARIAN RECIPES

Corn & Cheese Chile Rellenos

Preparation time: 30 minutes

Cooking time: 65 minutes

Servings: 8-12

Ingredients:

- Pellet: hardwood, maple
- 2 lbs. Ripe tomatoes, chopped
- Four cloves garlic, chopped
- 1/2 cup sweet onion, chopped
- One jalapeno stemmed, seeded, and chopped
- Eight large green new Mexican or poblano chiles
- Three ears sweet corn, husked
- 1/2 tsp. Dry oregano, Mexican, crumbled
- 1 tsp. ground cumin
- 1 tsp. Mild Chile powder
- 1/8 tsp. Ground cinnamon
- Salt and freshly ground pepper
- 3 cups grated Monterey jack
- 1/2 cup Mexican crema
- 1 cup queso fresco, crumbled
- Fresh cilantro leaves

Directions:

1. Place the tomatoes, garlic, onions and jalapeno in a shallow baking dish and place it on the grill grate before starting. This vegetable will expose more wood smoke.
2. When prepared to cook, start the grill on Smoke with the lid open until the fire is established (4 to 5 minutes). S
3. Mix the cooled tomato mixture in a blender and liquefy. Put in a pot.
4. Stir in the cumin, oregano, some chile powder, cinnamon, and some salt and pepper to taste.
5. Carefully peel the New Mexican chiles' blistered outer skin: Leave the stem ends intact and try not to tear the flesh.
6. Cut the corn off the cobs and put it in a large mixing bowl.
7. Bake or cook the Rellenos for 25 to 30 minutes or until the filling is bubbling and the cheese has melted.
8. Sprinkle with queso fresco and garnish it with fresh cilantro leaves, if desired. Enjoy!

Nutrition: Calories: 206 Carbs: 5g Fat: 14g Protein: 9g

Roasted Tomatoes with Hot Pepper Sauce

Preparation time: 20 minutes

Cooking time: 90 minutes

Servings: 4-6

Ingredients:

- Pellet: hardwood, alder
- 2 lbs. roman fresh tomatoes
- 3 tbsps. parsley, chopped
- 2 tbsps. garlic, chopped
- Black pepper, to taste
- 1/2 cup olive oil
- Hot pepper, to taste
- 1 lb. spaghetti or other pasta

Directions:

1. Prepare and ready to cook, set the temperature to 400degrees F and preheat, lid closed for 15 minutes
2. Rinse with water the tomatoes and cut them in half, length width and then place them in a baking dish cut side up.
3. Sprinkle with chopped parsley, garlic, then add salt and black pepper, and then pour 1/4 cup of olive oil over them.
4. Place on pre-heated and bake for 1 1/2 hours and then tomatoes will shrink, and the skins will be partly blackened.
5. Take the tomatoes from the baking dish and place them in a food processor, leaving the cooking oil and puree them.
6. Put the pasta into boiling salted water and cook until tender. Then drain and mix immediately with the pureed tomatoes.
7. Add the remaining 1/4 cup of raw olive oil and crumbled hot red pepper to taste. Toss and serve. Enjoy!

Nutrition: Calories: 111 Carbs: 5g Fat: 11g Protein: 1g

Grilled Fingerling Potato Salad

Preparation time: 15 minutes

Cooking time: 15 minutes

Servings: 6-8

Ingredients:

- Pellet: hardwood, pecan
- 1-1/2 lbs. Fingerling potatoes cut in half lengthwise
- Ten scallions
- 2/3 cup Evo (extra virgin olive oil), divided use
- 2 tbsps. rice vinegar
- 2 tsp. lemon juice
- One small jalapeno, sliced
- 2 tsp. kosher salt

Directions:

1. Prepare and ready to cook, turn temperature to High and preheat, lid closed for 15 minutes.
2. Brush the spring onions with the oil and place them on the grill. Cook for about 2-3 minutes until they are slightly charred. Remove and let cool. Once the spring onions have cooled, slice them and set aside.
3. Brush the Fingerlings with oil (reserving 1/3 cup for later use), then salt and pepper. Place cut side down on the grill cooked through, about 4-5 minutes.
4. In a bowl, mix the remaining 1/3 cup of olive oil, rice vinegar, salt, and lemon juice, then mix the green onions, potatoes and slices jalapeno.
5. Season with salt and pepper and serve. Enjoy!

Nutrition: Calories: 270 Carbs: 18g Fat: 18g Protein: 3g

Smoked Jalapeño Poppers

Preparation time: 15 minutes

Cooking time: 60 minutes

Servings: 4-6

Ingredients:

- Pellet: hardwood, mesquite
- 12 medium jalapeños
- Six slices bacon, cut in half
- 8 oz. cream cheese, softened
- 1 cup cheese, grated
- 2 tbsps. pork & poultry rub

Directions:

1. Prepare and ready to cook, turn temperature up to 180 degrees F and preheat, lid closed for 15 minutes.
2. Cut jalapeños in half lengthwise. Remove the seeds and ribs.
3. Combine softened cream cheese with Pork & Poultry rub and grated cheese.
4. Divide the mixture over each jalapeño half. Wrap in bacon and secure with a toothpick.
5. Put the jalapeños on a rimmed baking sheet. Place on the grill and smoke for 30 minutes.
6. Increase the temperature of the grill to 375 encores and cook for another 30 minutes or until the bacon is cooked to the desired doneness. Serve hot, enjoy!

Nutrition: Calories: 280 Carbs: 24g Fat: 19g Protein: 4g

Grilled Veggie Sandwich

Preparation time: 30 minutes

Cooking time: 30 minutes

Servings: 4-6

Ingredients:

- Pellet: hardwood, pecan
- Smoked hummus
- 1-1/2 cups chickpeas
- 1/3 cup tahini
- 1 tbsp. minced garlic
- 2 tbsps. olive oil
- 1 tsp. kosher salt
- 4 tbsps. lemon juice
- Grilled veggie sandwich
- One small eggplant, sliced into strips
- One small zucchini, cut into strips
- One small yellow squash, sliced into strips
- Two large Portobello mushrooms
- Olive oil
- Salt and pepper to taste
- Two heirloom tomatoes, sliced
- One bunch of basil leaves pulled
- Four ciabatta buns
- 1/2 cup ricotta
- Juice of 1 lemon
- One garlic clove minced
- Salt and pepper to taste

Directions:

1. Ready to cook, turn temperature to 180 degrees F and preheat, lid closed for 15 minutes.
2. In a prepared bowl of a food processor, combine the smoked chickpeas, tahini, garlic, olive oil, salt and lemon juice and blend until smooth but not completely smooth. Transfer to a bowl and reserve.
3. Increase grill temp to high (400-500 degrees F).
4. While the vegetables are cooking, mix the ricotta, the lemon juice, garlic, salt and some pepper.
5. Cut the ciabatta buns in half and then open them up—spread the hummus on one side and ricotta on the other. Stack the grilled veggies and top with tomatoes and basil. Enjoy!

Nutrition: Calories: 376 Carbs: 57g Fat: 16g Protein: 10g

Smoked Healthy Cabbage

Preparation time: 10 minutes

Cooking time: 2 hours

Servings: 5

Ingredients:

- Pellet: maple pellets
- One head cabbage, cored
- 4 tbsp. butter
- 2 tbsp. rendered bacon fat
- One chicken bouillon cube
- 1 tsp. fresh ground black pepper
- One garlic clove, minced

Directions:

1. Pre-heat your smoker to 240 degrees Fahrenheit using your preferred wood
2. Fill the hole of your cored cabbage with butter, bouillon cube, bacon fat, pepper, and garlic
3. Wrap the cabbage in foil about two-thirds of the way up
4. Make sure to leave the top open
5. Transfer to your smoker rack and smoke for 2 hours
6. Unwrap and enjoy!

Nutrition: Calories: 231 Fats: 10g Carbs: 26g Fiber: 1g

Garlic and Rosemary Potato Wedges

Preparation time: 15 minutes

Cooking time: 1 hour 30 minutes

Servings: 4

Ingredients:

- Pellet: maple pellets
- 4-6 large russet potatoes, cut into wedges
- ¼ cup olive oil
- Two garlic cloves, minced
- 2 tbsp. rosemary leaves, chopped
- 2 tsp. salt
- 1 tsp. fresh ground black pepper
- 1 tsp. sugar
- 1 tsp. onion powder

Directions:

1. Pre-heat your smoker to 250 degrees Fahrenheit using maple wood
2. Take a large bowl and add potatoes and olive oil
3. Toss well
4. Take another small bowl and stir garlic, salt, rosemary, pepper, sugar, onion powder
5. Sprinkle the mix on all sides of the potato wedge
6. Transfer the seasoned wedge to your smoker rack and smoke for one and a ½ hours
7. Serve and enjoy!

Nutrition: Calories: 291 Fats: 10g Carbs: 46g Fiber: 2g

Smoked Tomato and Mozzarella Dip

Preparation time: 5 minutes

Cooking time: 1 hour

Servings: 4

Ingredients:

- Pellet: mesquite
- 8 ounces smoked mozzarella cheese, shredded
- 8 ounces Colby cheese, shredded
- ½ cup parmesan cheese, grated
- 1 cup sour cream
- 1 cup sun-dried tomatoes
- 1 and ½ tsp. salt
- 1 tsp. fresh ground pepper
- 1 tsp. dried basil
- 1 tsp. dried oregano
- 1 tsp. red pepper flakes
- One garlic clove, minced
- ½ teaspoon onion powder
- French toast, serving

Directions:

1. Pre-heat your smoker to 275 degrees Fahrenheit using your preferred wood
2. Take a large bowl and stir in the cheeses, tomatoes, pepper, salt, basil, oregano, red pepper flakes, garlic, and onion powder and mix well
3. Transfer the mix to a small metal pan and transfer to a smoker
4. Smoke for 1 hour
5. Serve with toasted French bread Enjoy!

Nutrition: Calories: 174 Fats: 11g Carbs: 15g Fiber: 2g

Feisty Roasted Cauliflower

Preparation time: 15 minutes

Cooking time: 10 minutes

Servings: 4

Ingredients:

- Pellet: maple
- One cauliflower head, cut into florets
- 1 tbsp. oil
- 1 cup parmesan, grated
- Two garlic cloves, crushed
- ½ teaspoon pepper
- ½ teaspoon salt
- ¼ teaspoon paprika

Directions:

1. Pre-heat your Smoker to 180 degrees F
2. Transfer florets to smoker and smoke for 1 hour
3. Take a bowl and add all ingredients except cheese
4. Once smoking is done, remove florets
5. Increase temperature to 450 degrees F, brush florets with the brush, and transfer to grill
6. Smoke for 10 minutes more
7. Sprinkle cheese on top and let them sit (Lid closed) until cheese melts
8. Serve and enjoy!

Nutrition: Calories: 45 Fats: 2g Carbs: 7g Fiber: 1g

Savory Applesauce on the Grill

Preparation Time: 0 minutes

Cooking Time: 45 minutes

Servings: 2

Ingredients:

- 1½ pounds whole apples
- Salt

Directions:

1. Start the coals or turn a gas grill for medium direct cooking. Just make sure the grates are clean.
2. Put the apples on the grill directly over the fire. Close the lid and cook until the fruit feels soft when gently squeezed with tongs, 10 to 20 minutes total, depending on their size. Move to a cutting board and then let sit until cool enough to touch.
3. Cut the flesh from around the core of each apple; discard the cores. Put the chunks in a blender or food processor and process until smooth, or put them in a bowl and purée with an immersion blender until as chunky or smooth as you like. Add some salt and then taste adjusts the seasoning. Serve or refrigerate in a container for up to 3 days.

Nutrition: Calories: 15 Fats: 0 g Cholesterol: 0 mg Carbohydrates: 3 g Fiber: 0 g Sugars: 3 g Proteins: 0 g

VEGAN RECIPES

Wood Pellet Smoked Acorn Squash

Preparation Time: 10 minutes

Cooking Time: 2 hours

Servings: 6

Ingredients:

- 3 tbsp. olive oil
- 3 acorn squash, halved and seeded
- 1/4 cup unsalted butter
- 1/4 cup brown Sugar:
- 1 tbsp. cinnamon, ground
- 1 tbsp. chili powder
- 1 tbsp. nutmeg, ground

Directions:

1. Brush olive oil on the acorn squash cut sides then covers the halves with foil. Poke holes on the foil to allow steam and smoke through.
2. Fire up the wood pellet to 225°F and smoke the squash for 1 ½-2 hours.
3. Remove the squash from the smoker and allow it to sit.
4. Meanwhile, melt butter, Sugar: and spices in a saucepan. Stir well to combine.
5. Remove the foil from the squash and spoon the butter mixture in each squash half. Enjoy.

Nutrition: Calories: 149 Total Fat: 10g Saturated Fat: 5g Total Carbs: 14g Net Carbs: 12g Protein: 2g Sugar: 0g Fiber: 2g Sodium: 19mg Potassium: 0mg

Wood Pellet Smoked Vegetables

Preparation Time: 5 minutes

Cooking Time: 15 minutes

Servings: 6

Ingredients:

- 1 ear corn, fresh, husks and silk strands removed
- 1 yellow squash, sliced
- 1 red onion, cut into wedges
- 1 green pepper, cut into strips
- 1 red pepper, cut into strips
- 1 yellow pepper, cut into strips
- 1 cup mushrooms, halved
- 2 tbsp. oil
- 2 tbsp. chicken seasoning

Directions:

1. Soak the pecan wood pellets in water for an hour. Remove the pellets from water and fill the smoker box with the wet pellets.
2. Place the smoker box under the grill and close the lid. Heat the grill on high heat for 10 minutes or until smoke starts coming out from the wood chips.
3. Meanwhile, toss the veggies in oil and seasonings then transfer them into a grill basket.
4. Grill for 10 minutes while turning occasionally. Serve and enjoy.

Nutrition: Calories: 97 Total Fat: 5g Saturated Fat: 2g Total Carbs: 11g Net Carbs: 8g Protein: 2g Sugar: 1g Fiber: 3g Sodium: 251mg Potassium: 171mg

RED MEAT RECIPES

Red Wine Braised Lamb

Preparation Time: 10 minutes

Cooking Time: 4 hours

Servings: 6

Ingredients:

1. Rib rub—any of your choice
2. Lamb shanks—4
3. Red wine—1 cup
4. Beef broth—1 cup
5. Olive oil—as per your choice
6. Thyme—4 sprigs, fresh
7. Rosemary—4 sprigs, fresh

Directions:

1. Use the rib rub to coat the shanks of lamb properly.
2. Prepare your Wood Pellet Smoker-Grill by preheating it to a high temperature as per factory instructions. Close the top lid and leave for 12–18 minutes.
3. Transfer the shanks straight to the grilling grate and cook them for about 19–20 minutes.
4. Put the cooked shanks in a large Dutch oven and fill it with beef broth, herbs, and wine. Put the lid on the Dutch oven and transfer it to your smoker-grill. This time, reduce the cooking temperature to about 325degrees F.
5. Let the shanks cook for about 3–4 hours. Its internal temperature should reach about 180degrees F.
6. Take out and serve the shanks with the juices.

Nutrition: Calories: 160 Carbohydrate—13 g Protein—19 g Fat—4 g Sodium—440 mg Cholesterol—48 mg

Mustard Anchovy Rib Eye Steaks

Preparation Time: 10 minutes

Cooking Time: 2 hours12 minutes

Servings: 6

Ingredients:

- Ribeye—4 steaks, about 1-inch thick
- Garlic powder—1 tsp.
- Dry mustard—1 tbsp.
- Black pepper—2 tsp.
- Onion powder—2 tsp.
- Brown sugar—1 tbsp.
- Warm water—2 tbsps.
- Anchovy—10 fillets, minced

Directions:

1. Take a large enough bowl to mix everything except the steaks.
2. Use the prepared paste to coat the steaks on all sides. Put the steaks in your refrigerator to marinate for at least 2 hours.
3. Prepare your Wood Pellet Smoker-Grill by preheating it to a high temperature as per factory instructions. Close the top lid and leave for about 12–18 minutes.
4. Put the steaks on the grilling grate and cook for about 5 minutes on each side.
5. Once the internal temperature reaches 135degrees F, remove the steaks from the smoker-grill and let them cool down for 10 minutes.
6. Your dish is ready to be served.

Nutrition: Calories: 634 Carbohydrate—34 g Protein—67 g Fat—13 g Sodium—786 mg Cholesterol—160 mg

BAKING RECIPES

Baked Pumpkin Seeds

Preparation Time: 15 minutes

Cooking Time: 45 minutes

Servings: 10

Ingredients:

- 10 cups pumpkin seeds
- 4 teaspoons melted butter
- Java steak dry rub

Directions:

1. Set your wood pellet grill to smoke.
2. Preheat it to 300 degrees F.
3. Toss the seeds in steak rub and butter.
4. Place seeds
5. Cook for 45 minutes, stirring occasionally.

Nutrition: Calories: 170 Cal Fat: 15 g Carbohydrates: 4 g Protein: 9 g Fiber: 2g

Cinnamon Pumpkin Seeds

Preparation Time: 5 minutes

Cooking Time: 20-25 minutes

Servings: 8

Ingredients:

- 8 cups pumpkin seeds
- 2 tablespoons melted butter
- 2 tablespoons sugar
- 1 teaspoon ground cinnamon

Directions:

1. Set your wood pellet grill to smoke.
2. Preheat it to 350 degrees F.
3. Toss the pumpkin seeds in the butter, sugar and cinnamon.
4. Spread in a baking pan.
5. Roast for 20 to 25 minutes.

Nutrition: Calories: 285 Cal Fat: 12 g Carbohydrates: 34 g Protein: 12 g Fiber: 12 g

Cilantro and Lime Corn

Preparation Time: 15 minutes

Cooking Time: 15 minutes

Servings: 4

Ingredients:

- 4 corn cobs
- 1 tablespoon lime juice
- 2 tablespoons melted butter
- Smoked paprika
- 1 cup cilantro, chopped

Directions:

1. Preheat your wood pellet grill to 400 degrees F.
2. Grill for 15 minutes, rotating every 5 minutes.
3. Brush the corn cobs with a mixture of lime juice and butter.
4. Season with the paprika.

Nutrition: Calories: 100 Cal Fat: 2 g Carbohydrates: 19 g Protein: 3 g Fiber: 2 g

CHEESE AND BREAD

Berry Cobbler on a traeger grill

Preparation Time: 15 minutes

Cooking Time: 35 minutes

Servings: 8

Ingredients

For fruit filling

- 3 cups frozen mixed berries
- lemon juice
- 1 cup brown sugar
- 1 tbsp vanilla extract
- 1 tbsp lemon zest, finely grated
- A pinch of salt

For cobbler topping

- 1-1/2 cups all-purpose flour
- 1-1/2 tbsp baking powder
- 3 tbsp sugar, granulated
- 1/2 tbsp salt
- 8 tbsp cold butter
- 1/2 cup sour cream
- 2 tbsp raw sugar

Directions:

1. Set your traeger grill on "smoke" for about 4-5 minutes with the lid open until fire establishes and your grill starts smoking.
2. Preheat your grill to 350 oF for about 10-15 minutes with the grill lid closed.
3. Meanwhile, combine frozen mixed berries, Lemon juice, brown sugar, vanilla, lemon zest and pinch of salt. Transfer into a skillet and let the fruit sit and thaw.
4. Mix flour, baking powder, sugar, and salt in a bowl, medium. Cut cold butter into peas sizes using a pastry blender then add to the mixture. Stir to mix everything together.
5. Stir in sour cream until dough starts coming together.

6. Pinch small pieces of dough and place over the fruit until fully covered. Splash the top with raw sugar.
7. Now place the skillet directly on the grill grate, close the lid and cook for about 35 minutes until juices bubble, and a golden-brown dough topping.
8. Remove the skillet from the traeger grill and cool for several minutes.
9. Scoop and serve warm.

Nutrition: Calories 371, Total fat 13g, Saturated fat 8g, Total carbs 60g, Net carbs 58g, Protein 3g, Sugars 39g, Fiber 2g, Sodium 269mg, Potassium 123mg

Traeger Grill Apple Crisp

Preparation Time: 20 minutes

Cooking Time: 1 hour

Servings: 15

Ingredients

- Apples
- 10 large apples
- 1/2 cup flour
- 1 cup sugar, dark brown
- 1/2 tbsp cinnamon
- 1/2 cup butter slices
- Crisp
- 3 cups oatmeal, old-fashioned
- 1-1/2 cups softened butter, salted
- 1-1/2 tbsp cinnamon
- 1 cups brown sugar

Directions:

1. Preheat your grill to 350 oF.
2. Wash, peel, core, and dice the apples into cubes, medium-size
3. Mix together flour, dark brown sugar, and cinnamon then toss with your apple cubes.
4. Spray a baking pan, 10x13", with cooking spray then place apples inside. Top with butter slices.
5. Mix all crisp ingredients in a medium bowl until well combined. Place the mixture over the apples.
6. Place on the grill and cook for about 1-hour checking after every 15-20 minutes to ensure cooking is even. Do not place it on the hottest grill part.
7. Remove and let sit for about 20-25 minutes
8. It's very warm.

Nutrition: Calories 528, Total fat 26g, Saturated fat 16g, Total carbs 75g, Net carbs 70g, Protein 4g, Sugars 51g, Fiber 5g, Sodium 209mg, Potassium 122mg

APPETIZERS AND SIDES

Mushrooms Stuffed with Crab Meat

Preparation Time: 20 minutes

Cooking Time: 30-45 minutes

Servings: 4-6

Recommended pellet: Optional

Ingredients:

- 6 medium-sized portobello mushrooms
- Extra virgin olive oil
- 1/3 Grated parmesan cheese cup
- Club Beat Staffing:
- 8 oz fresh crab meat or canned or imitation crab meat
- 2 tablespoons extra virgin olive oil
- 1/3 Chopped celery
- Chopped red peppers
- ½ cup chopped green onion
- ½ cup Italian breadcrumbs
- ½ Cup mayonnaise
- 8 oz cream cheese at room temperature
- 1/2 teaspoon of garlic
- 1 tablespoon dried parsley
- Grated parmesan cheese cup
- 1 1 teaspoon of Old Bay seasoning
- ¼ teaspoon of kosher salt
- ¼ teaspoon black pepper

Directions:

1. Clean the mushroom cap with a damp paper towel. Cut off the stem and save it.
2. Remove the brown gills from the bottom of the mushroom cap with a spoon and discard.
3. Prepare crab meat stuffing. If you are using canned crab meat, drain, rinse, and remove shellfish.
4. Heat the olive oil in a frying pan over medium high heat. Add celery, peppers and green onions and fry for 5 minutes. Set aside for cooling.
5. Gently pour the chilled sauteed vegetables and the remaining ingredients into a large bowl.
6. Cover and refrigerate crab meat stuffing until ready to use.
7. Put the crab mixture in each mushroom cap and make a mound in the center.
8. Sprinkle extra virgin olive oil and sprinkle parmesan cheese on each stuffed mushroom cap. Put the mushrooms in a 10 x 15-inch baking dish.

9. Use the pellets to set the wood pellet smoker grill to indirect heating and preheat to 375 ° F.
10. Bake for 30-45 minutes until the filling becomes hot (165 degrees Fahrenheit as measured by an instant-read digital thermometer) and the mushrooms begin to release juice.

Nutrition: Calories 77, Total fat 1g, Saturated fat 1g, Total carbs 17g, Net carbs 15g, Protein 3g, Sugars 6g, Fiber 2g, Sodium 14mg, Potassium 243mg

Bacon Wrapped with Asparagus

Preparation Time: 15 minutes

Cooking Time: 25-30 minutes

Servings: 4-6

Recommended pellet: Optional

Ingredients:

- 1-pound fresh thick asparagus (15-20 spears)
- Extra virgin olive oil
- 5 sliced bacon
- 1 teaspoon of Western Love or salted pepper

Directions:

1. Cut off the wooden ends of the asparagus and make them all the same length.
2. Divide the asparagus into a bundle of three spears and split with olive oil. Wrap each bundle with a piece of bacon, then dust with seasonings or salt pepper for seasoning.
3. Set the wood pellet smoker grill for indirect cooking and place a Teflon coated fiberglass mat on the grate (to prevent asparagus from sticking to the grate grate). Preheat to 400 degrees Fahrenheit using all types of pellets. The grill can be preheated during asparagus Preparation Guide.
4. Bake the asparagus wrapped in bacon for 25-30 minutes until the asparagus is soft and the bacon is cooked and crispy.

Nutrition: Calories 77, Total fat 1g, Saturated fat 1g, Total carbs 17g, Net carbs 15g, Protein 3g, Sugars 6g, Fiber 2g, Sodium 14mg, Potassium 243mg

Bacon Cheddar Slider

Preparation Time: 30 minutes

Cooking Time: 15 minutes

Servings: 6-10 (1-2 sliders each as an appetizer)

Recommended pellet: Optional

Ingredients:

- 1-pound ground beef (80% lean)
- 1/2 teaspoon of garlic salt
- 1/2 teaspoon salt
- 1/2 teaspoon of garlic
- 1/2 teaspoon onion
- 1/2 teaspoon black pepper
- 6 bacon slices, cut in half
- ½Cup mayonnaise
- 2 teaspoons of creamy wasabi (optional)
- 6 (1 oz) sliced sharp cheddar cheese, cut in half (optional)
- Sliced red onion
- ½Cup sliced kosher dill pickles
- 12 mini breads sliced horizontally
- Ketchup

Directions:

1. Place ground beef, garlic salt, seasoned salt, garlic powder, onion powder and black hupe pepper in a medium bowl.
2. Divide the meat mixture into 12 equal parts, shape into small thin round patties (about 2 ounces each) and save.
3. Cook the bacon on medium heat over medium heat for 5-8 minutes until crunchy. Set aside.
4. To make the sauce, mix the mayonnaise and horseradish in a small bowl, if used.
5. Set up a wood pellet smoker grill for direct cooking to use griddle accessories. Contact the manufacturer to see if there is a griddle accessory that works with the wooden pellet smoker grill.
6. Spray a cooking spray on the griddle cooking surface for best non-stick results.
7. Preheat wood pellet smoker grill to 350 ° F using selected pellets. Griddle surface should be approximately 400 ° F.
8. Grill the putty for 3-4 minutes each until the internal temperature reaches 160 ° F.
9. If necessary, place a sharp cheddar cheese slice on each patty while the patty is on the griddle or after the patty is removed from the griddle. Place a small amount of mayonnaise mixture, a slice of red onion, and a hamburger pate in the lower half of each roll. Pickled slices, bacon, and ketchup.

Nutrition: Calories 77, Total fat 1g, Saturated fat 1g, Total carbs 17g, Net carbs 15g, Protein 3g, Sugars 6g, Fiber 2g, Sodium 14mg, Potassium 243mg

MORE SIDES

Cranberry-Almond Broccoli Salad

Preparation Time: 10 Minutes

Cooking Time: 60 Minutes

Servings: 8

Ingredients:

- ¼ - cup finely chopped red onion
- 1/3 - cup canola mayonnaise
- 3 - tablespoons 2% reduced-fat Greek yogurt
- 1 - tablespoon cider vinegar
- 1 - tablespoon honey
- ¼ - teaspoon salt
- ¼ - teaspoon freshly ground black pepper
- 4 - cups coarsely chopped broccoli florets
- 1/3 - cup slivered almonds, toasted
- 1/3 - cup reduced-sugar dried cranberries
- 4 - center-cut bacon slices, cooked and crumbled

Directions:

1. Absorb red onion cold water for 5 minutes; channel.
2. Consolidate mayonnaise and then 5 fixings (through pepper), blending admirably with a whisk. Mix in red onion, broccoli, and remaining fixings. Spread and chill 1 hour before serving.

Nutrition: Calories 104 Fat 5.9g Carb 11g Sugars 5g

Onion Bacon Ring

Preparation Time: 10 Minutes

Cooking Time: 1 Hour and 30 Minutes

Servings: 6 to 8

Ingredients:

- 2 large Onions, cut into ½ inch slices
- 1 Package of Bacon
- 1 tsp. of Honey
- 1 tbsp. Mustard, yellow
- 1 tbsp. Garlic chili sauce

Direction:

1. Wrap Bacon around onion rings. Wrap until you out of bacon. Place on skewers.
2. Preheat the grill to 400F with closed lid.
3. In the meantime, on a bowl combine the mustard and garlic chili sauce. Add honey and stir well.
4. Grill the onion bacon rings for 1 h and 30 minutes. Flip once.
5. Serve with the sauce and enjoy!

Nutrition: Calories: 90 Protein: 2g Carbs: 9g Fat: 7g

Grilled Watermelon juice

Preparation Time: 10 Minutes

Cooking Time: 15 Minutes

Servings: 4

Ingredients:

- 2 Limes
- 2 tbsp. oil
- ½ Watermelon, sliced into wedges
- ¼ Tsp. Pepper flakes
- 2 tbsp. Salt

Directions:

1. Preheat the grill to high with closed lid.
2. Brush the watermelon with oil. Grill for 15 minutes. Flip once.
3. In a blender mix the salt and pepper flakes until combined.
4. Transfer the watermelon on a plate.
5. Serve and enjoy!

Nutrition: Calories: 40 Protein: 1g Carbs: 10g Fat: 0

SNACKS

Smoked Guacamole

Preparation Time: 25 Minutes

Cooking Time: 30 Minutes

Servings: 6 to 8

Ingredients:

- ¼ cup chopped Cilantro
- 7 Avocados, peeled and seeded
- ¼ cup chopped Onion, red
- ¼ cup chopped tomato
- 3 ears corn
- 1 tsp. of Chile Powder
- 1 tsp. of Cumin
- 2 tbsp. of Lime juice
- 1 tbsp. minced Garlic
- 1 Chile, poblano
- Black pepper and salt to taste

Directions:

1. Preheat the grill to 180F with closed lid.
2. Smoke the avocado for 10 min.
3. Set the avocados aside and increase the temperature of the girl to high.
4. Once heated grill the corn and chili. Roast for 20 minutes.
5. Cut the corn. Set aside. Place the chili in a bowl. Cover with a plastic wrap and let it sit for about 10 minutes. Peel the chili and dice. Add it to the kernels.
6. In a bowl mash the avocados, leave few chunks. Add the remaining ingredients and mix.
7. Serve right away because it is best eaten fresh. Enjoy!

Nutrition: Calories: 51 Protein: 1g Carbs: 3g Fat: 4.5g

Jalapeno Poppers

Preparation Time: 15 Minutes

Cooking Time: 60 Minutes

Servings: 4 to 6

Ingredients:

- 6 Bacon slices halved
- 12 Jalapenos, medium
- 1 cup grated Cheese
- 8 oz. softened Cream cheese
- 2 tbsp. Poultry seasoning

Directions:

1. Preheat the grill to 180F with closed lid.
2. Cut the jalapenos lengthwise. Clean them from the ribs and seeds.
3. Mix the poultry seasoning, grated cheese, and cream cheese.
4. Fill each jalapeno with the mixture and wrap with 1 half bacon. Place a toothpick to secure it. Place them on a baking sheet and smoke and grill 20 minutes.
5. Increase the temperature of the grill to 375F. Cook for 30 minutes more.
6. Serve and enjoy!

Nutrition: Calories: 60 Protein: 4g Carbs: 2g Fat: 8g

Pellet: Mesquite

DESSERT RECIPE

Pellet Grill Apple Crisp

Preparation Time: 20 Minutes

Cooking Time: 60 Minutes

Servings: 15

Ingredients:

- Apples
- Ten large apples
- 1/2 cup flour
- 1cup sugar, dark brown
- 1/2 tbsp cinnamon
- 1/2 cup butter slices
- Crisp
- 3cups oatmeal, old-fashioned
- 1-1/2 cups softened butter, salted
- 1-1/2 tbsp cinnamon
- 2cups brown sugar

Directions:

1. Preheat your grill to 350.
2. Wash, peel, core, and dice the apples into cubes, medium-size
3. Mix flour, dark brown sugar, and cinnamon, then toss with your apple cubes.
4. Spray a baking pan, 10x13", with cooking spray, then place apples inside. Top with butter slices.
5. Mix all crisp ingredients in a medium bowl until well combined. Place the mixture over the apples.
6. Place on the grill and cook for about 1-hour checking after every 15-20 minutes to ensure cooking is even. Do not place it on the hottest grill part.
7. Remove and let sit for about 20-25 minutes
8. It's very warm.

Nutrition: Calories: 528 Total Fat: 26g Total Carbs: 75g Protein: 4g Sugars: 51g Fiber: 5g Sodium: 209mg

Fromage Macaroni and Cheese

Preparation Time: 30 Minutes

Cooking Time: 1 Hour

Servings: 8

Ingredients:

- ¼ c. all-purpose flour
- ½ stick butter
- Butter, for greasing
- One-pound cooked elbow macaroni
- One c. grated Parmesan
- 8 ounces cream cheese
- Two c. shredded Monterey Jack
- 3 t. garlic powder
- Two t. salt
- One t. pepper
- Two c. shredded Cheddar, divided
- Three c. milk

Directions:

1. Add the butter to a pot and melt. Mix in the flour. Stir constantly for a minute. Mix in the pepper, salt, garlic powder, and milk. Let it boil.
2. After lowering the heat, let it simmer for about 5 mins, or until it has thickened. Remove from the heat.
3. Mix in the cream cheese, parmesan, Monterey Jack, and 1 ½ c. of cheddar. Stir everything until melted. Fold in the pasta.
4. Add wood pellets to your smoker and keep your cooker's startup procedure. Preheat your smoker, with your lid closed, until it reaches 225.
5. Butter a 9" x 13" baking pan. Pour the macaroni mixture into the pan and lay on the grill. Cover and allow it to smoke for an hour, or until it has become bubbly. Top the macaroni with the rest of the cheddar during the last
6. Serve.

Nutrition: Calories: 180 Carbs: 19g Fat: 8g Protein: 8g

Spicy Barbecue Pecans

Preparation Time: 15 Minutes

Cooking Time: 1 Hour

Servings: 2

Ingredients:

- 2 ½ t. garlic powder
- 16 ounces raw pecan halves
- One t. onion powder
- One t. pepper
- Two t. salt
- One t. dried thyme
- Butter, for greasing
- 3 T. melted butter

Directions:

1. Add wood pellets to your smoker and follow your cooker's startup method.
2. Preheat your smoker, with your lid closed, until it reaches 225.
3. Cover and smoke for an hour, flipping the nuts one. Make sure the nuts are toasted and heated. They should be removed from the grill.
4. Set aside to cool and dry.

Nutrition: Calories: 150 Carbs: 16g Fat: 9g Protein: 1g

SAUCES AND RUBS

Classic Home-Made Worcestershire Sauce

Preparation Time: 10 minutes

Cooking Time: 15 minutes

Serving: 4

Ingredients

- ½ a cup of apple cider vinegar
- 2 tablespoons of water
- 2 tablespoon of coconut aminos
- ¼ teaspoon of mustard seeds
- ¼ teaspoon of onion powder
- ¼ teaspoon of garlic powder
- 1/8 teaspoon of cinnamon
- 1/8 teaspoon of black pepper

Directions:

1. Add all the listed ingredients to your saucepan
2. Bring it to a boil and stir well
3. Simmer for a few minutes
4. Remove the heat and allow it to cool
5. Use as needed!

Nutrition: Calories: 10 Carbs: 7g Protein: 2g

Original Ketchup

Preparation Time: 10 minutes

Cooking Time: 20 minutes

Serving: 4

Ingredients

- ½ a cup of chopped pitted dates
- 1 can of 6-ounce tomato paste
- 1 can of 14-ounce diced tomatoes
- 2 tablespoon of coconut vinegar
- ½ a cup of bone broth
- 1 teaspoon of garlic powder
- 1 teaspoon of onion powder
- 1 teaspoon of salt
- ½ a teaspoon of cayenne pepper

Directions:

1. Add the ingredients to a small-sized saucepan
2. Cook on medium-low for 20 minutes
3. Remove the heat
4. Take an immersion blender and blend the mixture until smooth
5. Remove the mixer and simmer on low for 10 minutes
6. Use as needed

Nutrition: Calories: 10 Carbs: 7g Protein: 2g

Lovely Mayonnaise

Preparation Time: 10 minutes

Cooking Time: Nil

Serving: 4

Ingredients

- 1 whole egg
- ½ a teaspoon of sea salt
- ½ a teaspoon of ground mustard
- 1 and a ¼ cup of extra light olive oil
- 1 tablespoon of lemon juice

Directions:

1. Place the egg, ground mustard, salt and ¼ cup of olive oil into a food processor
2. Whirl on low until mixed
3. While the processor is running, drizzle remaining olive oil and keep whirling for 3 minutes
4. Add lemon juice and pulse on low until thoroughly mixed
5. Chill for 30 minutes
6. Use as needed

Nutrition: Calories: 10 Carbs: 7g Protein: 2g

NUT AND FRUIT RECIPES

Grilled Fruit and Cream

Preparation Time: 15 minutes

Cooking Time: 10 minutes

Servings: 4

Ingredients:

- 2 apricots halved
- 1 nectarine halved
- 2 peaches halved
- ¼ cup blueberries
- ½ cup raspberries
- 2 tablespoons honey
- 1 orange, peel
- 2 cups cream
- ½ cup balsamic vinegar

Directions:

1. Preheat your smoker to 400 degrees F, lid closed
2. Grill peaches, nectarines, apricots for 4 minutes, each side
3. Place pan on the stove and turn on medium heat
4. Add two tablespoons honey, vinegar, orange peel
5. Simmer until medium-thick
6. Add honey and cream in a bowl and whip until it reaches a soft form
7. Place fruits on serving plate and sprinkle berries, drizzle balsamic reduction
8. Serve with cream and enjoy!

Nutrition: Calories: 230 Fats: 3g Carbs: 35g Fiber: 2g

TRADITIONAL RECIPES

Chicken Casserole

Preparation Time: 15 minutes

Cooking Time: 55 minutes

Servings: 8

Ingredients:

- 2 (15-ounce) cans cream of chicken soup
- 2 cups milk
- 2 tablespoons unsalted butter
- ¼ cup all-purpose flour
- 1 pound skinless, boneless chicken thighs, chopped
- ½ cup hatch chiles, chopped
- 2 medium onions, chopped
- 1 tablespoon fresh thyme, chopped
- Salt and ground black pepper, as required
- 1 cup cooked bacon, chopped
- 1 cup tater tots

Directions:

1. Preheat the Traeger grill & Smoker on grill setting to 400 degrees F.
2. In a large bowl, mix together chicken soup and milk.
3. In a skillet, melt butter over medium heat.
4. Slowly, add flour and cook for about 1-2 minutes or until smooth, stirring continuously.
5. Slowly, add soup mixture, beating continuously until smooth.
6. Cook until mixture starts to thicken, stirring continuously.
7. Stir in remaining ingredients except bacon and simmer for about 10-15 minutes.
8. Stir in bacon and transfer mixture into a 2½-quart casserole dish.
9. Place tater tots on top of casserole evenly.
10. Arrange the pan onto the grill and cook for about 30-35 minutes.
11. Serve hot.

Nutrition: Calories 440 Total Fat 25.8 g Saturated Fat 9.3 g Cholesterol 86 mg Sodium 1565 mg Total Carbs 22.2 g Fiber 1.5 g Sugar 4.6 g Protein 28.9 g

SAUCES, RUBS, AND MARINATES

Chimichurri Sauce

Preparation Time: 5 minutes

Cooking Time: 0 minute

Servings: 2

Ingredients:

- ½ cup extra-virgin olive oil
- One bunch of fresh parsley stems removed
- One bunch of fresh cilantro stems removed
- One small red onion, chopped
- 3 tbsp. dried oregano
- 1 tbsp. minced garlic
- Juice of 1 lemon
- 2 tbsp. red wine vinegar
- 1 tsp. salt
- 1 tsp. freshly ground black pepper
- 1 tsp. cayenne pepper

Directions:

1. Using a blender or processor, combine all of the ingredients and pulse several times until finely chopped.
2. The chimichurri sauce will keep in an airtight container in the refrigerator for up to 5 days.

Nutrition: Calories: 51 Carbs: 1g Fat: 5g Protein: 1g

RUBS, INJECTABLES, MARINADES, AND MOPS

Sweet and Spicy Cinnamon Rub

Preparation Time: 10 Minutes

Cooking Time: 0 Minutes

Servings: ¼ Cup

Ingredients:

- 2 tablespoons light brown sugar
- 1 teaspoon coarse kosher salt
- 1 teaspoon garlic powder
- 1 teaspoon onion powder
- 1 teaspoon sweet paprika
- ½ teaspoon freshly ground black pepper
- ½ teaspoon cayenne pepper
- ½ teaspoon dried oregano leaves
- ½ teaspoon ground ginger
- ½ teaspoon ground cumin
- ¼ teaspoon smoked paprika
- ¼ teaspoon ground cinnamon
- ¼ teaspoon ground coriander
- ¼ teaspoon chili powder

Directions:

1. In a small airtight container or zip-top bag, combine the brown sugar, salt, garlic powder, onion powder, sweet paprika, black pepper, cayenne, oregano, ginger, cumin, smoked paprika, cinnamon, coriander, and chili powder. Close the container and shake to mix. Unused rub will keep in an
2. airtight container for months.

Nutrition: Calories: 10 Carbs: 6g Protein: 1g

Wood-Fired Burger Shake

Preparation Time: 10 Minutes

Cooking Time: 0 Minutes

Servings: ¼ Cup

Ingredients:

- 1 teaspoon coarse kosher salt
- 1 teaspoon garlic powder
- 1 teaspoon dried minced onion
- 1 teaspoon onion powder
- 1 teaspoon freshly ground black pepper
- ½ teaspoon sweet paprika
- ¼ teaspoon mustard powder
- ¼ teaspoon celery seed

Directions:

1. In a small airtight container or zip-top bag, combine the salt, garlic powder, minced onion, onion powder, black pepper, sweet paprika, mustard powder, and celery seed. Close the container and shake to mix. Unused burger shake will keep in an airtight container for months.

Nutrition: Calories: 10 Carbs: 6g Protein: 1g

OTHER RECIPES YOU NEVER THOUGHT ABOUT TO GRILL

Wild Boar

Preparation Time: 20 minutes

Cooking Time: 6 hours

Servings: 4

Ingredients:

- 1 (4 pounds) wild boar roast
- 2 cups BBQ sauce
- Marinade:
- 1 tbsp chopped fresh thyme
- 1/3 cup honey
- One-fourth cup soy sauce
- One-fourth tsp cayenne pepper
- One-half tsp oregano
- One-fourth cup balsamic vinegar
- One-half tsp garlic powder
- 1 cup apple juice

Directions:

1. Roast the wild boar at 350 F for approximately 20 minutes or until internal temperature reaches 145 degrees Fahrenheit.
2. While the meat is cooking, combine all ingredients for the marinade in a bowl.
3. Marinate the meat for 6 hours in the refrigerator.
4. Drain the meat from the marinade.
5. Pour the marinade over the roast, cover, and cook on low for 5-6 hours
6. Serve with roasted potatoes.

Nutrition: Energy (calories): 388 kcal Protein: 40.35 g Fat: 5.5 g Carbohydrates: 44.5 g Calcium, Ca94 mg Magnesium, Mg105 mg Phosphorus, P320 mg Iron, Fe3.27 mg Fiber3.3 g

Honey Apricot Smoked Lamb Shank

Preparation Time: 1 hour

Cooking Time: 3-4 Hours

Servings: 6 Servings

Ingredients:

- 3 pounds of Whole lamb shank
- 1 cup of olive oil
- Glaze Ingredients
- 1/2 cup honey
- The ½ cup of orange juice concentrate
- 1/2 cup soy sauce
- 1/2 cup apricot jams
- 1 teaspoon ground nutmeg
- 1/2 teaspoon ground cloves

Directions:

1. Take a large mixing bowl and combine all the glaze ingredients in it.
2. Brush the lamb shank generously with the glaze mixture.
3. Marinate the lamb shank a few hours before cooking.
4. Preheat the smoker grill at a high Temperature until the smoke form.
5. Put the lamb on to the electrical smoker grate and cook for 3-4 hour at 220 degrees. Fahrenheit, or until the internal temperate reaches 150 degrees.
6. After every 30 minutes, baste the lamb shank with the glaze.
7. Enjoy!

Nutrition: Energy (calories): 833 kcal Protein: 48.58 g Fat: 50.28 g Carbohydrates: 48.31 g Calcium, Ca29 mg Magnesium, Mg77 mg Phosphorus, P470 mg Iron, Fe4.84 mg

Braised Rabbit and Red Wine Stew

Preparation Time: 30 minutes

Cooking Time: 2 hours

Servings: 4-6 servings

Ingredients:

- 1 skinless rabbit, chopped into pieces (3-lb, 1.4-kgs)
- Olive oil – 1 tablespoon
- Salted butter – 2 tablespoons
- 1 yellow onion, peeled and chopped
- 1 celery stalk, peeled and chopped
- 1 carrot, peeled and chopped
- 2 garlic cloves, peeled and minced
- Flour – 2 tablespoons
- Chicken broth – 4 cups
- Dry red wine – 1 cup
- 1 thyme sprig
- 2 bay leaves
- Salt and black pepper – to taste
- Crusty baguette – to serve

Directions:

1. Warm the olive oil in a Dutch oven over moderately high heat. Add the rabbit pieces to the pot in batches and cook until browned and golden. Set the meat to one side.
2. Melt the butter in the same pot and add the onion, celery, and carrot. Sauté for 10-12 minutes until soft. Add the garlic and sauté for another 60 seconds.
3. Sprinkle over the flour and stir well to combine, cook for 60 more seconds.
4. Next, pour in the chicken broth and red wine. Return the meat to the pot along with the thyme and bay leaves and bring to a simmer.
5. Cover the Traeger oven with a lid and place on the grill. Cook for approximately 2 hours until the rabbit is cooked through and tender. Season with salt and pepper to taste.
6. Serve with crusty bread.

Nutrition: Energy (calories): 407 kcal Protein: 42.07 g Fat: 21.69 g Carbohydrates: 6.56 g Calcium, Ca40 mg Magnesium, Mg40 mg Phosphorus, P288 mg Iron, Fe2.48 mg Fiber0.8 g

Citrus Smoked Goose Breast

Preparation Time: 45 minutes

Cooking Time: 3 hours

Servings: 8 servings

Ingredients:

- 8 goose breast halves
- Freshly squeezed orange juice – ½ cup
- Olive oil one-third cup
- Dijon mustard one-third cup
- Brown sugar one-third cup
- Soy sauce one-fourth cup
- Runny honey one-fourth cup
- Dried onion, minced 1 tablespoon
- Garlic powder 1 teaspoon

Directions:

1. In a bowl, combine the marinade ingredients and whisk until combined. Coat the goose with the marinade. Cover the bowl and transfer to the fridge for between 3-6 hours.
2. Transfer the goose to the grill, occasionally brushing with the marinade for the first half an hour, before discarding any excess marinade.
3. Continue cooking until the bird's juices run clear and when using a meat thermometer, registers an internal Smoke Temperature of 165°F (74°C), approximately 10-15 minutes.

Nutrition: Energy (calories): 1173 kcal Protein: 158.84 g Fat: 38.28 g Carbohydrates: 53.18 g Calcium, Ca60 mg Magnesium, Mg225 mg Phosphorus, P1723 mg Iron, Fe38.69 mg

Maple-Glazed Pheasants

Preparation Time: 3 hours

Cooking Time: 17 hours

Servings: 6 servings

Ingredients:

- 2 whole pheasants (2.5-lb, 1.1-kgs each)
- Brown sugar – ¼ cup
- Kosher salt – ¼ cup
- Water – 4 cups
- Maple syrup – 2 cups

Directions:

1. First, make the brine. Dissolve the sugar and salt in the water.
2. Arrange the pheasant in a large container and pour over the brine mixture. If the birds are not entirely covered, pour over more water.
3. Chill overnight (8-12 hours).
4. Take the birds out of the liquid and pat dry using kitchen paper. Set aside to dry for an hour.
5. Place the pheasants in the smoker.
6. In the meantime, add the maple syrup to a pan over moderately high heat and boil down until thick and syrupy.
7. After the meat has been smoking for an hour, baste the birds with the maple syrup. Continue to base the meat every half an hour.
8. Enjoy warm or allow to cool.

Nutrition: Energy (calories): 620 kcal Protein: 55.36 g Fat: 8.6 g Carbohydrates: 79.38 g Calcium, Ca164 mg Magnesium, Mg73 mg Phosphorus, P542 mg Iron, Fe2.92 mg

Ultimate Duck Breasts

Preparation Time: 5 minutes

Cooking Time: 20 minutes

Servings: 6

Ingredients:

- 6 skin-on, boneless duck breasts (7.5-oz, 210-gms each)
- Turbinado sugar – ¼ cup
- Kosher salt – one-eight cup
- Garlic powder – 3/4 tablespoon
- Light brown sugar 1/3 cup
- Paprika – 1½ tablespoons
- Onion powder 3/4 tablespoon
- Lemon pepper – 1/2 tablespoon
- Black pepper – 1/2 tablespoon
- Dried thyme – 1/2 tablespoon
- Chili powder – 1 teaspoon
- Cumin – 1/2 tablespoon

Direction

1. Rinse the duck breasts and gently pat dry with kitchen paper.
2. Score the fat layer in a crisscross pattern using a sharp knife.
3. Combine all rub ingredients in a small bowl.
4. Flip the duck breasts over so that they are sitting fat-side down and coat the non-fat side liberally with the Prepared rub.
5. Arrange one or two duck breasts at a time on the grill, skin side down, and cook for approximately 5 minutes until a brown crust has developed. Once you have rendered as much fat as possible, turn the duck over.
6. Cook for a few more minutes, until medium rare.
7. Allow the meat to rest for several minutes before slicing and serving.
8. Serve.

Nutrition: Energy (calories): 142 kcal Protein: 6.85 g Fat: 2.76 g Carbohydrates: 23.62 g Calcium, Ca42 mg Magnesium, Mg11 mg Phosphorus, P19mg Iron, Fe1.77 mg

Wild Game Chili

Preparation Time: 50 minutes

Cooking Time: 6 hours

Servings: 8-12 servings

Ingredients:

- 3 slices of bacon, chopped
- Venison or wild hog, ground into small cubes (3-lb, 1.4-kgs)
- 1 large onion, peeled, finely chopped
- Beer
- Canned chopped green chilies
- Cumin seeds, crushed – 1 tablespoon
- Chili seasoning mix, of choice 2/3 cup
- Tomato juice
- Hot pepper sauce – 1 tablespoon
- White cornmeal – ½ cup

Directions:

1. In a frying pan, sauté the bacon with the onions, until the bacon is just browned.
2. Add the game and sear all over.
3. In a pan, add 1½ cups of beer along with the green chilies, cumin, and chili mix, simmering until it is a gravy-like consistency.
4. Add the remaining beer followed by the tomato juice and hot pepper sauce.
5. Pour the mixture into a pan and transfer to the smoker.
6. Smoke-cook for between 4-6 hours.
7. Before serving, add the cornmeal and stir to thicken and combine.
8. Simmer for 20 minutes and serve with flour tortillas.

Nutrition: Energy (calories): 557 kcal Protein: 21.69 g Fat: 6.34 g Carbohydrates: 107.3 g Calcium, Ca43 mg Magnesium, Mg238 mg Phosphorus, P589 mg Iron, Fe3.73 mg Fiber10 g

Grilled Rabbit with Wine and Rosemary Marinade

Preparation Time: 10 minutes

Cooking Time: 40 minutes

Servings: 6

Ingredients:

- 1 rabbit cut into pieces
- For marinade
- 3 cloves of garlic, mashed
- 1 1/2 tsp rosemary
- 1 cup of white wine, dry
- 1/2 cup olive oil
- 1 tbsp white vinegar
- 1 tsp mustard
- 1/2 tsp cumin
- Salt and ground pepper to taste

Directions:

1. Whisk all marinade ingredients from the list.
2. Place the rabbit meat in marinade and toss to combine well.
3. Cover with plastic wrap and refrigerate for several hours (preferably overnight).
4. Remove meat from marinade and pat dry on a paper towel.
5. Set the Smoke Temperature to High.
6. Place the rabbit pieces directly on grill rack.
7. Grill for about 12 to 15 minutes per side.
8. The rabbit meat is ready when no longer pink inside and the juices run clear.
9. Serve hot.

Nutrition: Energy (calories): 269 kcal Protein: 15.45 g Fat: 22.29 g Carbohydrates: 1.4 g Calcium, Ca17 mg Magnesium, Mg14 mg Phosphorus, P121 mg Iron, Fe1.55 mg Fiber0.2 g

Grilled Wild Boar Steaks with Blueberry Sauce

Preparation Time: 40 minutes

Cooking Time: 1 hour

Servings: 6

Ingredients:

- 4 large steaks of wild boar
- For the marinade
- 2 glasses dry red wine
- Juice from 1 lemon, preferably organic
- 2 bay leaves
- 2 tbsp sweet paprika powder
- 1 cup fresh celery, finely chopped
- Salt and black pepper, crushed
- 1 tsp rosemary fresh or dry
- For the sauce
- 3/4 lbs. blueberries
- 1 tsp brown sugar
- Salt and white freshly ground pepper

Directions:

1. Combine the marinade ingredients together in a small food processor and juice the lemon into it.
2. Place the meat into a suitable container and pour the marinade over it; cover and set it in the refrigerator to marinate for at least 3 hours
3. Brush the marinade off the meat and place it on a grill.
4. Cook it over medium or medium-high heat, turning it regularly and basting it with the marinade.
5. Transfer it to a serving plate. Meanwhile, boil a pan of water with a teaspoon of salt for the blueberries; cook these to the desired consistency Add the sugar and simmer the sauce for about 5 minutes, until it has thickened; season it before serving.

Nutrition: Energy (calories): 2447 kcal Protein: 99.16 g Fat: 7.78 g Carbohydrates: 515.74 g Calcium, Ca160 mg Magnesium, Mg1190 mgPhosphorus, P2906 mg Iron, Fe13.89 mg Fiber43.6 g Sugars, total30.21 g

Grilled Wild Goose Breast in Beer Marinade

Preparation Time: 2 hours

Cooking Time: 50 minutes

Servings: 4

Ingredients:

- 4 goose breasts
- 2 cups beer of your choice
- 1 1/2 tsp Worcestershire sauce
- 1 tsp garlic powder
- 1/2 tsp paprika
- Salt and pepper

Directions:

1. Place the goose breasts in a Ziploc plastic bag.
2. Pour in the beer, Worcestershire sauce, garlic powder, paprika, and salt and pepper. Close the bag and shake to combine all ingredients well.
3. Marinate in refrigerated for 2 hours.
4. Remove the goose meat from marinade and pat dry on kitchen towel (reserve the marinade).
5. Place the goose breasts on the grate. Brush occasionally with the marinade only for the first half an hour.
6. Continue to cook for 10 - 15 minutes longer.
7. Serve hot.

Nutrition: Energy (calories): 905 kcal Protein: 155.25 g Fat: 25.61 g Carbohydrates: 6.48 g Calcium, Ca35 mg Magnesium, Mg195 mg Phosphorus, P1651 mg Iron, Fe37.86 mg Fiber0.4 g Sugars, total1.07 g

Grilled Wild Rabbit with Rosemary and Garlic

Preparation Time: 15 minutes

Cooking Time: 1 hour

Servings: 4

Ingredients:

- 1 - 2 wild rabbits (about 2 pounds)
- 2 cloves of garlic, melted
- 2 tbsp of rosemary dried, crushed
- Juice from 1 lemon
- 1/4 cup olive oil
- Salt and freshly ground pepper

Directions:

1. If we use a whole rabbit, cut up a rabbit by removing the front legs, which are not attached to the body by bone.
2. Slide your knife up from underneath, along the ribs, and slice through. Cut the trunk into slices of 4-5 cm thick.
3. In a bowl, mix the dry ingredients and lemon juice.
4. Brush the rabbit pieces with the garlic-rosemary mixtures.
5. Start the pellet grill to pre-heat to 300 degrees.
6. Lay the rabbit pieces onto grill rack.
7. Grill for about 12 - 15 minutes per side.
8. Serve.

Nutrition: Energy (calories): 733 kcal Protein: 25.22 g Fat: 15.42 g Carbohydrates: 128.9 g Calcium, Ca42 mg Magnesium, Mg303 mg Phosphorus, P740 mg Iron, Fe3.5 mg Fiber10.7 g Sugars, total4.57 g

Stuffed Wild Duck on Pellet Grill

Preparation Time: 2 hours

Cooking Time: 2 hours

Servings: 6

Ingredients:

- 1 wild duck (about 4 pounds), cleaned
- 1 mushroom cut into slices
- 1 tsp fresh parsley, finely chopped
- 1/2 tsp of thyme
- 1/4 cup fresh butter
- Salt and pepper

Directions:

1. Combine mushrooms, parsley, thyme, fresh butter and salt and pepper.
2. Place the mushrooms mixture in the wild duck belly.
3. On the pellet grill on Smoke with the lid open until the fire is established (4 to 5 minutes).
4. Set the Smoke Temperature to 350F and preheat, lid closed, for 10 to 15 minutes.
5. Place the duck directly on the grill grate.
6. Cover the grill and cook the duck for 1-1/2 hours.
7. After 1-1/2 hours, drain the juices and fat from the pan and flip the duck, breast side down.
8. Let the duck cool down, pull the twigs, and serve.

Nutrition: Energy (calories): 261 kcal Protein: 15.91 g Fat: 21.39 g Carbohydrates: 0.81 g Calcium, Ca8 mg Magnesium, Mg20 mg Phosphorus, P157 mg Iron, Fe3.83 mg Fiber0.2 g Sugars, total0.56 g

CONCLUSION

In conclusion, it is a fact that the Traeger pellet grill has made grilling easier and better for humanity, and Grilling, which is part of the so-called "dietetic" cooking, had been made easier through the Traeger grill. Giving us that tasty meal, we've been craving for and thus improving the quality of life. This book made you a lot of recipes that you can make at your home with your new Traeger Pellet grill. The recipes will give so much satisfaction with the tenderness and tasty BBQ.

The Traeger barbecues are electrical, and a typical 3-position function controls them. A cylindrical device transmits the pellets from the storage to the fire place, like a pellet stove. Traeger Grill smoker promotes an excellent outcome for your meat and other recipes. This smoker provides a tasty for your foods. To achieve such a real taste, you need the quality of materials and get the exact smoking. It is best if you get the maximum consistency of smoking so that you can have the best result of your meat and other recipes. Moreover, if you add more flavors to your recipes, use the best wood pellet for cooking for your food.

Many people ask me questions on why I chose Traeger pellet grill, and you might think, well, the answer is clear and true, and yes! It's right before us. Why?

It cooks with a wood fire, giving an excellent quality in taste because nothing is like it: real wood, real smoking, natural aroma. In terms of the cooking process, it has changed a lot. Experts chefs tend to have new experiments with new flavor and ingredients to create a delicious and tasty recipe.

Grilling is one of the most popular cooking processes that grant a perfect taste to your recipes. Grilling is a much healthier method than others because its benefits food, preserves flavor, and nutrients. But from the other side, a Traeger grill smoker's wood pellet grill allows you to grill your food quickly and with less effort and smoke. The advantage of having a Traeger grill smoker in your home is the versatility, helps you cook food faster, provides a monitoring scale for the temperature, and it is one of the essential parts of cooking.

It is a versatile barbecue. In fact, it can be grilled, smoked, baked, roasted, and stewed—everything you can imagine cooking with the Traeger grill smoker. You will find that this Traeger grill smoker is a flexible tool that has a good service.

As we all could testify that using the pellet grill has been made simple by Traeger: its intuitive control panel has a power button and a knob that allows you to adjust the temperature comfortably.

Finally, we need to note that through Grilling, we can always find new flavors in our dishes: with Traeger pellets, you can smoke your dishes, giving them an ever new and different flavor. Traeger Grill smoker is the answer you are looking for your taste buds. Don't waste your time and have your own smoker at home and start cooking your favorite recipes with this book.

CPSIA information can be obtained
at www.ICGtesting.com
Printed in the USA
BVHW060044090221
599629BV00001B/17

9 781801 650335